# Happy About Customer Service?

## Creating a Culture of Customer Service Excellence

Do not W/D. On reading list - 2015-16

## By Ken Welsh

D1637902

about.info

20660 Stevens Creek Blvd.
Suite 210
Cupertino, CA 95014

# Happy About Customer Service?: Creating a Culture of Customer Service Excellence

Copyright © 2008 by Ken Welsh

First Printing: September 2008
Paperback ISBN: 978-1-60005-093-0
Place of Publication: Silicon Valley, California, USA
Paperback Library of Congress Number: 2008921964

eBook ISBN: 978-1-60005-094-7

## Trademarks

All terms mentioned in this book that are known to be trademarks or service marks have been appropriately capitalized. Happy About® cannot attest to the accuracy of this information. Use of a term in this book should not be regarded as affecting the validity of any trademark or service mark.

## Warning and Disclaimer

Every effort has been made to make this book as complete and as accurate as possible, but no warranty of fitness is implied. The information provided is on an "as is" basis. The authors and the publisher shall have neither liability nor responsibility to any person or entity with respect to any loss or damages arising from the information contained in this book.

# Endorsements of 'Happy About Customer Service'

*"We've all witnessed excellent customer service in our lives. 'Happy About Customer Service?' challenges leaders to bring out the best in their companies and themselves. If you're looking for a book to inspire you to do better, far better, in customer service, this is the book for you."*

**Simon Nynens, Chairman and CEO, Wayside Technologies Group, Inc.**

*"I just read this book and it is great. I love it! It will be a great tool for us and any other company who has the good sense to read it and apply."*

**Courtney Wight, Customer Service Manager, Headsets.com, Inc.**

*"Ken speaks directly to us in this book and provides us with all the tools to make a difference in the lives of our customers, and thus enhance our businesses, and consequently our own lives."*

**Michele Brandenburger, Class Act Productions, East London, South Africa**

*"Ken Welsh was one of the key catalysts that turned me from a terrified amateur at Toastmasters to a professional public speaker and TV presenter on Channel 9. He helped me to develop my message and then worked on how I could deliver it in a more meaningful way"*

**Chris Gray, CEO of Red Wealth Creations, a Presenter on "My Home" Channel 9 Sydney and author of 'Go for Your Life'**

*"Ken Welsh's approach to customer service focuses on getting back to the basics of communication. Our business focuses on selling technology products and services over the phone, so verbal communication is key. Ken has worked with our sales organization for nearly a year now and our sales reps have benefited by applying the techniques and skills he's taught."*

**Shawn Giordano, Senior Director of Sales, Programmer's Paradise**

## Author

- By Ken Welsh
  http://www.letstalkcommunication.com

## Publisher

- Mitchell Levy
  http://www.happyabout.info

## Teclarity

- Teclarity
  http://www.teclarity.com

## Dedication

Clichéd as it may sound and real as it is -
To my amazing partner Francesca and my parents, Don and Marcia, for their tireless support, encouragement and faith.

## Acknowledgement

This book could never have been written without the trust, support and friendship of Mike Faith and his amazing team at Headsets.com.

To me, this company represents the absolute benchmark in Customer Service—Mike calls it "Customer Love"—and that is exactly what it is. I encourage every Customer-oriented company to aspire to achieve what Headsets.com now takes as second nature.

Without the trust of my friends, for they are much more than mere clients, at Headsets.com, many of my techniques would have gone untested.

Here's to the incredible Customer Service standards set by one of the world's leaders in Service Excellence.

Thank you, Mike & Headsets.com.

And of course, without the amazing assistance, foresight, and tolerance of Mitchell Levy, Tom Pencek and their team at "Happy About", I could never have succeeded at writing this thank you for making this book possible.

# A Message from Happy About®

Thank you for your purchase of this Happy About book. It is available online at http://www.happyabout.info/customerservice.php or at other online and physical bookstores.

- Please contact us for quantity discounts at sales@happyabout.info
- If you want to be informed by e-mail of upcoming Happy About® books, please e-mail bookupdate@happyabout.info

Happy About is interested in you if you are an author who would like to submit a non-fiction book proposal or a corporation that would like to have a book written for you. Please contact us by e-mail editorial@happyabout.info or phone (1-408-257-3000).

Other Happy About books available include:

- They Made It:
  http://happyabout.info/theymadeit.php
- Happy About Online Networking:
  http://happyabout.info/onlinenetworking.php
- I'm on LinkedIn — Now What???:
  http://happyabout.info/linkedinhelp.php
- Tales From the Networking Community:
  http://happyabout.info/networking-community.php
- Scrappy Project Management:
  http://happyabout.info/scrappyabout/project-management.php
- 42 Rules of Marketing:
  http://happyabout.info/42rules/marketing.php
- Foolosophy:
  http://happyabout.info/foolosophy.php
- The Home Run Hitter's Guide to Fundraising:
  http://happyabout.info/homerun-fundraising.php
- Confessions of a Resilient Entrepreneur:
  http://happyabout.info/confessions-entrepreneur.php
- Memoirs of the Money Lady:
  http://happyabout.info/memoirs-money-lady.php
- 30-Day Bootcamp: Your Ultimate Life Makeover:
  http://happyabout.info/30daybootcamp/life-makeover.php
- The Business Rule Revolution:
  http://happyabout.info/business-rule-revolution.php
- Happy About Joint Venturing:
  http://happyabout.info/jointventuring.php

# contents

## Foreword by Mike Faith

Ken Welsh has been a mentor, trainer, and most valued consultant to my company, Headsets.com. Soon after we commenced putting Ken's teachings into practice, our Customer service staff started to enjoy their role more and to please Customers like never before. Customers loved the change, and our sales rose consistently.

The accolades followed: We were named in the Inc500 list of fastest-growing companies for three years running, and in 2006, won a prestigious Stevie Award for Best Customer Service Team. Ken Welsh's expertise enabled our company to achieve faster sales growth, more repeat business, happy Customers, increased profits, and a happier staff. Will *Happy About Customer Service* help your company enjoy these benefits as well? I say resoundingly, YES, YES, YES.

This book is an engaging read, and you could enjoy it for that reason alone. Most notably, it gets you thinking, then deciding, and then taking action. Ken leads you through the process, systematically. As you work through the book, Ken is by your side, teaching and asking key questions, helping you plan before you take action. The process is a proven fast-track method that will help you quickly achieve the positive changes that you want.

A simple, yet essential lesson I learned from Ken is this: "The quicker we get started, the quicker we enjoy the rewards." So, I recommend that you turn the page, enjoy the trip, *take action*, and start reaping the rewards.

Mike Faith
CEO Headsets.com, Inc.

# Using This Book to Create a Culture of Customer Service Excellence

A question for you: Are you Happy About Customer Service? Genuinely Happy About Customer Service? If you aren't certain, consider the quality of:

- The Service you receive
- The Service you give
- The Service that your Customers deserve

If your answer is yes, then congratulations. Read no further.

If your answer, like mine, is no, perhaps, or maybe—try this question:

Do you want to develop your Customer Service standards so that you consistently, and to the endless pleasure of your Customers, deliver Customer Service Excellence? If your answer to this is YES, MOST DEFINITELY YES, and it's because you want to:

- engender improved loyalty among existing Customers
- attract new Customers

- surpass your peers or competitors because no one will do what you do with the level of excellence that you do it

- give yourself and your team a real sense of success and fulfilment

- improve your bottom line

Then you, like me, have the motivation to improve yourself, your team, and your company. So, read on!

I believe that, in virtually every job or career, Customer Service is an essential element. We often don't consider the "big picture" of who our Customers really are. Customers aren't simply the people who buy from retail outlets. In some way, we are all Customers to each other, each day. Most of modern life is about Service, from dealing with our peers to helping our children to negotiating with our boss.

Because Customers are an intrinsic and essential part of our lives, my suggestion is to recognize their significance by making them a proper noun—that is, always put them in capital letters. You always use a capital when you write the name of a city, a country or a person's name, so why not do the same for things that are important to you? These words deserve to be proper nouns because they are essential components of your daily life on them: Customer, Customer Service, Customer Service Excellence. You'll note that throughout this book, I've used capitals to create a few new "proper nouns" for people and actions that I feel are important enough to warrant it.

Let's first consider the impact of Customer Service. How great does it feel when someone goes out of their way to be helpful and friendly? When they perform beyond your expectations?

For me, excellent Customer Service always makes an impression. It makes me feel that someone really cares, and that I am much more than merely "potential for profit." I leave the experience feeling so good that I want to do something to make someone else feel great.

Now think about the multiplier effect of this, because a Customer Service experience is, literally, more than the sum of its parts. If you deal with, say, 20 people each day, and they deal with maybe 20 people, who deal with 20 people, and so on....

Based on that equation, in one day you have the potential to affect (directly and indirectly) 8,000 people. This is why it's so important to give and receive the best Customer Service possible—because it makes such a difference in the lives of everyone around us.

Thank you for buying this book and for expressing an interest in improving Customer Service. This book will guide you in your quest to grow, to prosper, and to have fun doing it. Each chapter offers insight and ideas to help you constantly achieve Customer Service Excellence.

## Now It's Your Turn

For your first task, I'd like you to calculate how many people you are likely to affect in one week—make it a five-day week, to keep the math simple. (HINT: It isn't 8,000 x 5, it's much, much more)

The total number of people that I affect in 1 week is……………

Incredible, isn't it?

So, if you can affect that many people in one week, consider how many of those people are Customers, potential Customers, or know someone who could be a potential Customer. On a more esoteric level, it could be said that Customer Service makes a difference in not only isolated situations, but also in the world. I truly believe that by helping someone improve their day, the goodwill of that act will, undoubtedly, cascade down to others.

After many years as a business voice coach and Customer Service coach, it became overwhelmingly clear that, while there are many complex vocal, psychological, physiological, and other techniques for "dealing" with Customers, the most successful techniques all came down to this basic premise:

*Treat your Customers as you would like to be treated when you are a Customer.*

I like people and I like helping people. In that spirit, you'll find that much of this book is written as though I'm talking with you. Consequently, you'll notice that I use "us," "we," and "our," rather than "you" and "your." This is intentional. It's the way that I work with a company—we have to be in it together. So, from this point onwards, we are in it together—Welcome Aboard!

I firmly believe that people are a very valuable resource, and, more importantly, that every Customer is a person.

As Stanley Marcus (of Neiman Marcus fame) said:

*Consumers are Statistics.*
*Customers are people.*

But enough of my quest to make the world a better place. You can decide for yourself to pursue a similar goal, or you might focus on providing stellar Customer Service in order to improve your bottom line. Regardless, one thing is clear: Customer Service is becoming a key "discriminator" for purchase choice. People like being treated well and choose Customer-focused companies over non-Customer-focused companies when other factors are equal.

The purpose of this book is to expand on that premise in a simple, easy-to-implement way, providing a skill set to ensure that you and your team continually differentiate your company from others through the provision of constant and continually-improving Customer Service Excellence. You will discover how to offer genuine Customer Care, because Customers genuinely care.

In this book, I'll guide you through my concept of Customer Service Excellence in the same way I talk to my various clients when working with them face-to-face. If you have a question, turn on your computer, link to the Web, and send me an e-mail, or better yet, give me a call. To help you further, I've included a complementary link to a stand-alone PowerPoint Presentation that can be used as a simple memory jogger and training tool.

All of these techniques are "tried & true," with many of them used consistently by one of my favorite companies—San Francisco-based Headsets.com, one of the world leaders in true Customer Service Excellence.

This book can readily be used as a manual to help you create a culture of company-wide Customer Service Excellence. Each chapter concludes with a section ("Now It's Your Turn") for you to identify specific actions, objectives, or concepts to help you along the way. Write in the spaces provided and then turn these words into actions.

I've also issued a series of "challenges," asking you to put some of the concepts into practice for a period of time. I'd love to hear about your experiences, so I also invite you to e-mail me at the address below. While you're online, check out the resources available at **The Centre for Customer Service Excellence** (http://www.c4cse.com).

Many of the concepts and steps in this book will seem basic and easy to implement. If that is the case, I've done my job. You'll find that I repeat myself—and for good reason—because, clearly, the more often we hear, see, and do something, the faster it becomes habit and the sooner we will be able to adapt it to our unique circumstances.

Ultimately, this book is meant to enhance Customer loyalty, attract new Customers, and (hand-in-hand with good economic management) improve your bottom line—so that you and your Customers will be *Happy About Customer Service.*

## Chapter 1 Takeaways

1. This book will guide you in using Customer Service Excellence to achieve the following:

– Engender improved loyalty amongst existing Customers

– Attract new Customers

– Create a company with no peers or competitors, because no one will do what you do with your level of excellence and

– Give yourself and your team a real sense of success and fulfilment.

Customer Service has an immense cumulative effect. Consider how your contribution is part of the equation.

## Always Remember:

*Consumers are Statistics.*
*Customers are people.*

*Treat your Customers as you would like to be treated when you are a Customer.*

## NOW IT'S YOUR TURN   # 1

Let's establish a few starting points:

Who are you? (Please write down five words/short phrases that define who you are)

_____

_____

_____

_____

What does your company do?

_____

_____

_____

_____

What do you do in your company?

_____

_____

_____

_____

Happy About Customer Service?

What do you want to gain by using this book?

_____

_____

_____

_____

**What are you prepared to do to achieve Customer Service Excellence?**

_____

_____

_____

_____

_____

# 2

# Start with Your Customers in Mind & Be a Customer Yourself

## The Secret to Achieving Customer Service Excellence

*Treat Every Customer as You Would like to be treated when You are a Customer Yourself.*

With that basic premise in mind, let's expand on it together.

I'm often asked how to improve the bottom line of a company. My approach is to immediately direct my energy to improving the "top line": Company Culture, Management Style, and then, Customer Service Representatives.

Fundamentally, it is Company Culture that drives each and every person on our team.

Get this right, and the bottom line will look after itself.

If you ensure that all of your team are Customer Service Experts, (not simply CSRs), then your existing Customers will remain loyal, and you'll also attract new Customers. So, how do we improve your top line?

Let's review some of the early, big picture aspects of establishing a Customer Service Culture, which will help you enthusiastically retain existing Customers and attract new Customers.

The basic steps (without these you'll be pushing it uphill all the way):

## Consistently Lead from the Top

We must remember the significance of relationships within the company. After all, our Customer Service team members are essentially Customers themselves—management's Customers. If we expect our Customer Service Team to respect our Customers, we must show—clearly and unfailingly—the same respect from our Management Team. The goal is to lead by example and insist that middle management and supervisors maintain the same standards.

## Do Little Things Early—Rather than Big Things Late

Each step mentioned below this line will help achieve a company-wide culture of Customer Service Excellence. They can be introduced as major initiatives or incrementally through individual cells within the company, depending upon the existing company culture and the receptiveness of the team to change. However, in my opinion, one of the most powerful principles to apply to anything in any situation is to do little things early rather than big things late.

If something doesn't work out the way that we thought it would, look at it, admit that it didn't work, and then take steps to rectify it immediately. This rule applies equally to marketing initiatives, staffing appointments, language ideas, new techniques, and even internal gossip (though there shouldn't be any when we maintain positive communication).

However, I also advise to choose your "little things" carefully.

Imagine a company in which a staff member hasn't turned up at work for a few days. Gossip will start within a day or two if people aren't aware of what is happening.

So, what should we do?

Ignoring it would be a "little thing." However, this would simply permit the gossip to continue. Telling our team not to think or talk about it would be another "little thing," and again, this is likely to encourage people to think and talk about it.

My suggestion would be to get on the phone, find out what is happening, and then to trust our people and tell them what we can (this is covered by "Communicate, Communicate, Communicate," an item later in this section).

Likewise, if someone's performance in a specific field is lacking approach, follow the above advice as soon as the problem is identified, rather than leaving it until irreparable damage is done.

# Our Customers Know What They Want—so Let's Make Sure that We Do, Too

While some of our Customers' needs, wants, and desires are easy to predict (e.g., good value, great service, being treated with respect), other aspects may not be as obvious. Everyone carries their own unique needs. Consequently, it is essential to always look for new and innovative ways to find out what our Customers want.

Their wants will include how they want to contact us (face-to-face, by phone or Web), how they want us to contact them, how often they'd like us to contact them, how they'd prefer to pay us and, of course, how much they're prepared to pay.

And, while you're gathering these details, always remember to establish an understanding of the Customers' expectations (so we can exceed them):

At our disposal are a number of tools to discover what our Customers want, including inquiries by our Customer Service Team and the usual plethcra of surveys (online, mailed, telephone, etc). However, the real range of possibilities is as endless as your imagination. I've worked with some companies that simply used online survey forms, while others hold Customer lunches, dinner cruises, office and factory visits.

Regardless of how we do it, it is essential to do it—consistently, regularly, and with some variety in format. And, whenever possible, we should help our Customers feel part of the process, giving them a sense that they are important enough for us to want their input.

Sure, it may cost a bit more to determine our Customers' desires; however, in the long run, we're more likely to increase our bottom line through Customer Retention, Customer Loyalty, and the best marketing tool of all, Customer Referral. As well as this, we'll be able to better gauge what our Customers value, how much our Customers are prepared to pay for what extras, and how long they're prepared to wait for various products and services.

Great examples of this include:

- Airlines that charge more for extra leg room

- Software companies that use web downloads and e-mails for urgent software upgrades, saving large amounts of money on couriers and catering to the urgency of the Customers' needs

- Electronics retailers who courier mp3 players and yet only snail mail batteries because they know that their Customers aren't prepared to pay more for the shipping than the price of the product

It can even mean that we can hold lower levels of stock, when we find that our Customers are prepared to wait a couple of days, while we order less common replacement parts and accessories from the manufacturer, rather than us holding them in our own storage.

An example of this is some of the newer electronic products that give their users advanced warning of an impending battery replacement. Because our Customers' appliance gives them a 10-day warning, we can take 5 days to get them their replacement battery direct from the manufacturer and so reduce the storage space that we need to devote to these batteries.

Ultimately, knowing these types of thing can help us better manage our company by increasing margin and decrease our overheads.

## Choose the Best—and Be Prepared to Pay for It

This applies to employees, consultants, and training and techniques.

Remember that our Internal Customers are as important as our External ("paying") Customers. When we set high standards, it means we need to recruit the best, train with the best, and reward the best performance.

However, if we only consider monetary amounts as measures of performance and if we only establish a monetary-based reward mentality, we will never achieve the ultimate levels of Customer Service Excellence. It is essential that we get feedback from Customers on the level of Service Excellence achieved by our team. Then, we need to reward those who achieve the best of several measures, not simply our best "sales people." And just as we want our team to be inventive and find unique ways to exceed each Customer's expectations, our rewards also should be tailored to individual circumstances and our team's individual needs and desires.

## Measure, Monitor, and Measure Again

Once we've found out what Customers want, we need to gauge our success in catering to their needs and desires. This allows our team to set standards to meet and then exceed. Once we exceed these expectations, can we raise our standards and continually strive to improve our Customer Service?

Never forget, as Jim Collins put it in his book, *Good to Great*: "Good is the enemy of Great." So, once you've established your measures and standards, never settle for anything less than the best. And, always encourage your team to strive to exceed everyone's expectations—even their own. In other words, don't rest on your laurels. Once you achieve a good standard consistently, raise the bar and go for a great standard. And once you're great—go for fantastic.

# Catch and Reward

**(In contrast to "catch and release"—because we don't want to lose these great people)**

This also applies to rewards and praise for our Team and our Customers. The adage, "Catch people doing things right," should be ingrained as part of our culture in order to achieve Customer Service Excellence.

The quality of Service that can be provided is directly proportional to the energy and enthusiasm of an individual or a team. Consequently, anything that we can do to maintain this energy can result in improvements to our Customer Service.

The catch and reward can be as simple as, "The paperwork you do to schedule our team's annual leave is so fantastic. Our company could never be as successful as it is without that paperwork—how about you take the afternoon off as soon as you've completed it?"

A couple of examples:

A company that I work with regularly has always had good Customer Service and always had a supportive, friendly environment; however, on one visit I found that the energy was down. The team had become complacent about their work, their metrics, and, consequently, each other. Most of the team had been with the company for at least nine months, and they'd lost some of their enthusiasm. Not just for their work—for their fellow workers. This manifested in a relatively quiet workplace with no "buzz." More importantly, it was also beginning to show in the numbers—their Customer Service ratings had dropped and their sales were starting to be affected ever so slightly.

To stay in line with my principle of doing little things early rather than big things late, I immediately asked if we could try an experiment.

Without the knowledge of any other teams, I asked one team to make a point of complimenting anyone that they passed in the corridor for one week. Within three days, the place was buzzing again and everyone was complimenting everyone else.

I was asked to "pulse check" a company that I'd previously worked with. It had been a happy, friendly working environment that could easily recruit high caliber people and retain them because of the environment. Suddenly, they couldn't keep staff.

On my first day I simply observed. What caught my attention was a manager who turned a daily "walk-around"—originally designed to "catch people doing things right"—into a "find out what's going wrong" journey, and people had begun to dread seeing her in the morning.

I immediately asked her to compliment three people on each walk-around. Within one week, the energy was noticeably higher, and the Service rating and sales improved correspondingly. And with the next hiring campaign they had over fifty applicants for each position.

A simple step that cost nothing and made a big difference. Isn't that what we all want?

# Mind Your Language!

Language is the most powerful tool at our disposal. What we say influences how others perceive us and how we perceive ourselves.

Great Customer Service Language involves a number of basic attributes, all of which should instantly become part of your company's communication culture, both internally and externally:

- **Positive Language.** Use it with our Customers, about our Customers, and among our team. Simple things such as using "absolutely" or "perfect" rather than "okay" can make an incredible difference to how the recipient of our message feels and what they take from our conversation.

- **Welcoming Language.** Never forget to deliver a cheerful, positive "Welcome" and "Farewell" message. Simply put, thank people for calling you or meeting with you, and wish them well when they go.

- **Believable Language.** Maintain integrity in what you say and back it up with what you do. We must always believe in the language that we use and take ownership of it—customers can detect insincerity.

- **Trustworthy Language.** Make Promises and Keep them—there are no exceptions to this!

# Role Playing—Overt and Covert

To ensure that our team has every training advantage available, never underestimate the power of role-playing to prepare:

- our new recruits before they meet our Customers,

- anyone before an important meeting (internal or external), and

- seasoned team members for new initiatives and for regular "fine-tuning" of their work to help them continually advance.

Recognize the importance of knowing what our Customers are experiencing. This version of role-playing is sometimes called "mystery shopping" (usually using professional companies), and it can give us a "feel" for what's happening. However, it will never replace the "feel" that we will get if we can do it in person and share our Customer's experience.

When we call a call center, walk into a shop, eat at a restaurant, or take a flight, we should never underestimate the value of our experiences as a Customer. We can always learn from the great work being done out there in the real world. Write down every great Customer experience that you have, see how you can adapt it to your work environment, and make it even better!

# Communicate, Communicate, Communicate

Do this internally, externally—anywhere and everywhere.

As Leaders, we need to communicate our ideas, needs, and desires.

Concurrently, we need to keep our team "in the loop," and help them take ownership of where we are going and how we are all on the journey. A transparency of accountability and responsibility is absolutely essential in maintaining trust, morale, and a sense of ownership among our team.

Train with passion. Lead with passion. Recruit people who are passionate about Customer Service.

Remember: **Passion + Patience = Perfection**

Be Patient—perfection takes time!

# Chapter 2 Takeaways

To be certain of developing a Customer-Oriented Company Culture:

1. Consistently lead Customer Respect from the top.
2. Do Little Things Early—rather than big things late.
3. Listen to your Customers. They know what they want—so, let's make sure that we do, too.
4. "Catch and Reward"—catch our people doing great things and reward them for it.
5. Mind your language—consistently use positive, professional, and friendly language that inspires your team and encourages your Customers.
6. Communicate, Communicate, Communicate. Do this internally, externally, and any other "..... ally" that you can think of!

## Always Remember:

*Passion + Patience = Perfection*
*Be Patient—Perfection Takes Time!*

## NOW IT'S YOUR TURN   #2

What can you do to lead our team with passion?

_____

_____

_____

What can you do to find out what your Customers want and expect of us?

_____

_____

_____

_____

What are 5 exciting ways to reward your team?

_____

_____

_____

_____

Happy About Customer Service?

How can you apply "little things early" rather than "big things late"?

_____

_____

_____

_____

When will you start taking these steps?

_____

_____

_____

_____

# Our Customer Family

Now that you've established your Customer Service Culture, I'm going to join you on this journey, so from now on, in most instances, I'll refer to "our" Customers and "our" Team, rather than "yours."

## Our Customer Family Tree

Let's consider the starting point of Customer Service: our Customer Family Tree. Since most everyone that we meet is a Customer of some type, the branches of this tree should be familiar to us. It simply reflects the basic types of human relationships and includes the following levels of familiarity:

- Strangers

- Acquaintances

- Friends

- Family

One of our key objectives should be to help our Customers evolve from one level of familiarity to the next (i.e., from strangers to acquaintances to neighbors to friends, and ultimately, to family). In order to do this, we need to understand each level's characteristics, challenges, and desires.

# Strangers

### Definition

A person that we don't know.

### Description

A stranger doesn't know about us, nor us about them. They may not even know that our products or services exist.

### Characteristics

Strangers have little or no interest in us or our products until they find that they need or desire what we provide, and even then, they may not be able to find us or our company.

### Desires

A stranger's needs and desires may not initially relate to us or our company. However, circumstance often creates a need, desire, or curiosity for our services, which propels the stranger to discover them.

### Challenges

1. Introducing an awareness of our services to someone who has never heard of us or what we do.

2. Fostering a stranger's curiosity in our services.

3. Helping a stranger recognize their need for our services.

4. Creating a desire to have and use what we can give them.

# Acquaintances

## Definition

A person that we know slightly.

## Description

An acquaintance has little more than a passing interest in what we do or how we do it. They typically don't know that what we do could help them, or how.

They haven't used our services and will most likely "shop around" if they decide that they need what we offer.

## Characteristics

While acquaintances may be aware of our services, they have no reason to show loyalty because they have never used them. They don't even know why they should prefer us to anyone else.

## Desires

While a common factor for each acquaintance will be their desire for the best value for their money, each acquaintance's concept of "value" will be unique.

## Challenges

1. Determining each acquaintance's concept of value.
2. Convincing an acquaintance that we provide the best value for their money.
3. Encouraging an acquaintance to go directly to us without shopping around, or at least, coming back once they have shopped around.

# Friends

## Definition

A person that we know well and like.

## Description

Friends have used us before and are keen to find out more—and hopefully keen to use us again.

## Characteristics

A friend is someone who already trusts us. We've successfully worked with them before (meaning that it's been mutually enjoyable, beneficial, and profitable). If it wasn't successful, it's highly likely that they are no longer a friend, and we've managed to commit the cardinal sin of de-evolving a Customer.

## Desires

Like each of us, friends desire love. Friends are by choice—they can choose to stay with us or leave us. Just as in "real life," this is a relationship that we must always endeavor to maintain and improve. We've invested in them financially and emotionally—we can't afford to lose them. They've bought from us a few times and we've impressed them with our Service and services. They don't want to look elsewhere because they're comfortable with us, and their chief desire is to have their expectations continually and reliably met. They want to be satisfied. If we've done our job correctly, they may even tell their friends about us. In short, they have invested with us, financially and emotionally. And, to our advantage, they don't want to lose us, either.

## Challenges

1. Evolving friends to family. The best way we can help them evolve to "family" is to continually, reliably—and almost religiously—exceed their expectations!

2. When we've already been doing our best and set our friends' expectations high, finding new ways to exceed these expectations can be a major challenge. Be creative, be inventive, and ask your Customers how to do things better.

# Family

## Definition

People who are related to one another.

## Description

While we obviously can't literally restrict our Customer base to those who share our gene pool, we can have Customers who share the characteristics of "Family." We love these people because they love us, and they love us because we love them! They will stand by us through thick and thin.

We have deposited so much good will in their "Relationship Bank," that even if we make a mistake, they'll forgive us.

## Characteristics

Family knows us and what to expect from us; however, they still love to be surprised when we do even better than they expected.

They will stand by us, even if our services may not be the lowest price, because they see past the dollar value to the value of the ongoing relationship. This may be in terms of the special deals that we give our family, such as individualized Service from a person who knows their background and personal desires, a no-question return policy and on-going product support, or anything else that makes them feel "special."

We've treated them well previously, and they know that we'll treat them well in the future.

## Desires

They want us to do well—of course, this is partially because it means that they can do well. No matter how much we like to think altruistically, we are human, and they are human, and to be human means that we often act with self-interest. That may be harsh but true. If we consider things this way, it can give us a completely fresh perspective.

So, what does that basic piece of behavioral psychology mean in terms of Customer Service? It means that our family Customers want us to do well because:

- our success means that prices to them are less likely to increase,

- they can rely on us being in business for a long time, and they won't need to look around for a new supplier (don't we all like life to be simple and easy?), and

- they can boast to their friends and family that "I knew them when they were starting out" or "I get these great deals—you should see the special offers that I get as part of my loyalty program."

### Challenges

Genuinely exceeding our family's expectations can be quite a challenge, because every time that we deal with our Customers, we're trying to do our best (that's probably how these Customers became "Family"). Now we really have to "raise the stakes" and be creative so they can take pleasure in being our Customer, and become one of a very rare and special group—our *Blindly Proud Grandparents*.

## Blindly Proud Grandparents—How Fantastic are They?

As the fifth and ultimate level of Customer familiarity, a blindly proud grandparent is a Customer for whom we can do no wrong. They are unconditionally loyal and sing our praises so strongly, so adamantly, so consistently, that they do our marketing for us!

They are our greatest fans and always will be.

Some people may refer to these Customers as "champions"; however, to me, they are more than that. Here's my account:

I remember being in my grandparents' house when I was around five years old, pretending I could juggle (I had no coordination as a child—nor do I now, come to think of it). In my case, three balls and two five-year-old hands tended to mean one thing, and one thing only—one ball too many!

Ultimately, that one ball too many went rogue and hit an antique vase. To my five-year-old dismay, a loud crash left the prized vessel laid out like a jigsaw puzzle beside my grandparents' bed (which, incidentally, I was bouncing on as I tried to juggle).

My parents and grandparents rushed to my aid only to find me attempting to rebuild a porcelain jigsaw puzzle. I was about to be, let's say, severely reprimanded, when both of my grandparents simultaneously acknowledged that their once cherished antique vase was "a dirty old flower pot that they'd been meaning to get rid of."

That was an act of blindly proud grandparents. Now, do you see what I mean about them being more than our champions?

## Nurturing Our Customer Family

In this modern, Internet-based world, our potential Customers have more resources at their disposal than ever before.

Take my services as an example.

I work with a small group of Customers to whom I provide exclusive Service, no matter where they are in the world. Sometimes, I will fly to their country and work with them face-to-face, other times I will coach over the telephone or via webcam. If the work doesn't require the spontaneity of the spoken word, we may even resort to e-mails.

Videoconferencing is playing a larger part in my life. At times, I may ask a Customer to videotape their presentation and e-mail the file to me. Then, we'll review it online or by phone.

Most of my Customers readily use all of the above techniques; however, ultimately, face-to-face is always a great way to ensure that it all comes together. So, regardless of where they are in the world, I can jump on a plane and know that I can be in their office within a day (airlines' schedules and breakdowns permitting).

I don't advertise—people usually find me through family-level Customers, and, because of the level of trust in those relationships, my new Customers usually don't shop around. The principle behind this is that there is no point for them to shop around when we have no competition—no one can do for them what we can, as well as we can. Plus, it doesn't matter if I'm next door or a hemisphere away. I'm the one they choose over anyone else, because, in today's world, they can!

I've told you that a Customer can choose products and services from all over world. I've painted the picture of a competitive world where Customer choice rules. And, specifically, while many of us continually complain that our economies are bleak and that we can't afford "things"—we really can. The average household in the developed world is more prosperous than ever before.

Take something simple, like a cup of coffee. We now have more ways of making a cup of coffee than our forefathers had ways to start a fire.

We can buy:

- Instant Coffee

- Coffee pots

- Percolators

- Electric drip-o-lators

- Manual drip-o-lators

- Turkish Ibriqs

- French Cafeteires

- Italian Moka-Napoletana Stovetop Pots

- Electric espresso makers

- "Café Bar" instant espresso machines

- "Mr. Cappuccino" short-cut machines

- ...... I'm certain that you can name several more ......

So, what's the moral of all this?

Money = Choice

We live in an affluent society with enough money to let us make choices. We are human, and so we like to be able to choose. By exercising our prerogative to choose, we express our individuality, increase our self-esteem, and feel empowered.

How do we access this aspect of human nature to our best advantage? By recognizing the individuality and humanity of our Customers.

Increasingly, in our affluent world, Customers' choices are no longer solely governed by price. Clearly, price is considered; however, Customer choice is increasingly based on Service quality and personalization. This is where we can gain an immediate advantage over the companies who are stuck in the past, that is, companies who are still sitting, relishing their former glory as "the best discounter" rather than exploring the frontiers of Customer Service Excellence. As over the top as this may sound, I firmly believe that this is the new direction of "sales and Service," and, ultimately, a way that we can all make a difference to everyone concerned. Just consider how amazing it would be if everyone treated everyone else exactly as they like to be treated when they're a Customer!

Previously, Customer choice was largely price-based, and we had to cut costs to compete. Now, we have a tool that costs very little and gives us a major edge: Customer Service Excellence.

If pricing is within an acceptable range, it will be the quality of Customer Service that differentiates between suppliers. And as excellent—even amazing—Customer Service is largely based on our culture rather than our capital, we are immediately in a great place to create loyalty among existing Customers and to attract new ones, through minimal capital investment.

Our Customer Service is what will help us evolve strangers to acquaintances to friends. As a result, we will foster a family of loyal, supportive Customers and a select few Blindly Proud Grandparents.

With this in mind, let's start ensuring that our Customer Service is so amazing that we can confidently proclaim we have no competition—because no one else does what we do as well as we do it!

## Assisting Evolution

Back to Darwinism—or helping our Customers evolve to a higher level. Let's see if we can help move everyone up a few branches on our Customer familiarity tree.

To grow and develop in our increasingly competitive business world, survival of the fittest is definitely a consideration. And, like Darwin, we can look at each "species" individually and explore their needs and desires as unique attributes. However, unlike Darwin, we gain little by looking back on history, because our Customers' are searching and longing for more; their needs and desires are constantly changing and developing. We must project forward to help our Customer evolve. The future's truly progressive and successful businesses will anticipate what Customers want—before they know they want it.

To accomplish this, it is essential to recognize that each step in our Customers' evolution poses its own unique challenges, each with many solutions. As Customer Service experts, it is up to us to identify our Customers' needs and desires, understand our own unique set of circumstances, and assess our company culture to choose the most effective solutions.

The following sections provide a brief summary of possible challenges you will face when transitioning Customers from one level of familiarity to another. It also offers a selection of solutions as a template for our own set of solutions. There are clearly as many sets of challenges and solutions as there are Customers, so we need to be prepared to think before we act and to be creative in our approach.

# Strangers to Acquaintances

## *Challenges*

1. Introducing an awareness of our product or services to someone who has never heard of us or what we do.

2. Fostering a stranger's curiosity in our products or services.

3. Helping a stranger recognize their need for our services.

4. Creating a desire to have and use what we can give them.

## *Solutions*

- Advertise and market.

- Create a unique profile for ourselves.

- Create a "presence."

Advertising and marketing will provide incentives for strangers to develop into acquaintances, and for acquaintances to evolve into friends. There are numerous experts in these fields who have written books and given workshops specifically on these topics. My suggestion is that you check them out, look them up, and see what they have to offer. I also strongly suggest that you choose companies that you admire for their branding and marketing strategies, learn from what they do, and adapt them to our own unique circumstances. There's nothing like learning from other people's experience.

## Customer Transition Examples

Because the transition from Stranger to Acquaintance is all about awareness, the typical approach for these transitions is through marketing and/or promotional initiative. Consider the Restaurants on Lygon Street in Melbourne, Australia, noted for their ability to transition Strangers to Acquaintances through their own specific type of marketing.

As you walk along Lygon Street day or night, waiters and waitresses will stand outside their restaurants waiting to pounce on the unassuming stranger. They are trained to spot non-regulars to the area and to solicit them with descriptions of the "Dish of the Day" and the chef's specialty for the evening. Their mission is to entice passers by to be aware of their restaurant, to come in now, and if not now, to ask, "What are you doing for dinner later tonight?" or "Perhaps, supper after a show?"

In several areas of the Middle East this is taken even further. I can remember arriving by bus in Hurgahda, by the Red Sea in Egypt. (This is before it became today's major tourist resort.) The tourists were obvious, as they alighted the cross-country bus tired, dirty and dusty.

Throngs of local men touting the value of adjacent hotels greeted you with: "Warm shower, my friend—clean sheets, no bed bugs—very cheap." They were even delegated authority by the hotel owners to offer "A discount on the spot." Within two minutes, there would be a simple, efficient transition of this tired and dirty Stranger to an Acquaintance.

There is an even more interesting transition technique used in Middle Eastern cities when a tourist is spotted standing around, looking at a map. (Even without the map, I stood out as a tourist.) A man greeted me with, "Hey, mister, where you from?"

"Australia," was my simple reply. It was immediately met with:

"Sydney, Melbourne, Brisbane, Adelaide—maybe, you know my cousin—you want direction?"

Before I knew it, my newfound acquaintance, who had one cousin in Melbourne (or whatever city I wasn't from) had walked with me, guiding me to wherever it was I was trying to go, and suddenly, completely by chance (of course), we had stumbled upon his brother's perfume shop, and, of course, it would be an insult if we passed without having a cup of coffee.

Talking with other travelers, you realize that there is no offense here—it's simply part of the game in transitioning Strangers to Acquaintances. These acquaintances may never come back; however, they are likely to make that one-off purchase.

While I'd prefer not to fabricate cousins in far-off places, I mention these techniques to illustrate the broad range of approaches. We don't always have to stick with conventional advertising to reach new markets.

I would encourage slightly more subtlety and veracity in our approach to this transition because, ultimately, we'd like the opportunity to help our Strangers evolve all the way to the top of our Customer Family Tree.

# Acquaintances to Friends

## Challenges

1. Determining each acquaintance's concept of "value."

2. Convincing an acquaintance that we provide the best value for their money.

3. Encouraging an acquaintance to go directly to us without shopping around, or at least, coming back to us once they have shopped around.

## Solutions

- Bond with our acquaintances.

- Develop a keen understanding of their personal needs and desires.

- Make it easy for our acquaintances to deal with us—let them choose the method.

## Customer Transition Examples

For this transition to work, we are taking someone who has met us (and used our Services) once or twice, and now we're helping them to get to know us more. Personally, I would want to build my trust in the person/company. I'd want to know that they value me and remember me.

Let's look at an example of this type of transition that I experienced in San Francisco.

I'm fussy about coffee. I like my latte the way that I like my latte. In many parts of the U.S., it can be challenging to find espresso, let alone a good latte.

I spend a lot of time in San Francisco and have found some reasonably good coffee shops there. One day, a new coffee shop called "Dolce" opened near my apartment. I thought, "Hey, another coffee shop. At least, it's handy." That was all. Then, I walked past one day and noticed them installing an espresso machine and later a sign with the word "Illy." That was enough to say to me, these people are at least worth trying. They know a good brand of Italian coffee. So, try it I did. It was good.

A second time, and still good. This time "Steve" noticed my accent, asked me where I was from and what my name was. Now, every time I come in, they know me and that I'm Australian and they call me "Ken."

One time, on my first day back in San Francisco after being away for several months, I went in for a coffee and was greeted with a smile, a "Good to see you, Ken," and "You're back already."

I'll be back there again next weekend.

# Friends to Family

## Challenges

This transition represents two key challenges:

1. If our Customer Friends want their desires to be satisfied and their expectations to be met, the best way that we can help them evolve to Family is to continually, reliably—and almost religiously—exceed their expectations!

2. We must encourage our Internal Customers to continually put in the extra effort when they are already giving incredible Customer Service.

## Solutions

- When we've already been doing our best and have set our Friends expectations so high, finding new ways to exceed these expectations can be a major challenge—we need to be creative, inventive, and ask our Customers how we can do things better for them.

- Spend time with our Family.

- Talk with our Family—share experiences with them.

- Show trust and show that we can be trusted too.

- Put ourselves into our Customer Friends' place and try to find things that would please and surprise us, if we were them.

## Customer Transition Examples

We're really starting to raise the stakes here; however, there are still lots of examples of successfully transitioning Friends to Family.

On a small backstreet in Dubai, there is an Arab sweet shop. Great Arabian coffee scented with cardamom and a selection of sugary, syrupy sweets to make a dentist's wallet smile.

I was taken there by a local friend who frequents the shop. Through this introduction, I very quickly leapt through the lower branches of the Customer Family Tree. Being introduced by someone already at the Family level is a big plus, so always remember the power of the personal referral.

Within one day, I was Mr. Ken, and the whole team knew my taste in coffee. Then, a seemingly simple thing happened. Mustafa was busy when we arrived, and he had business to talk with my friend. He simply beckoned me past the counter and, pointing to the kitchen, said, "See what's fresh."

Suddenly, with that extra trust, I had jumped all the way to Family.

Continuing along the theme of coffee—referring back to my coffee shop experience in San Francisco—recently, I returned to Dolce. I was greeted, as usual, with a smile and a: "Hi, Ken! Are you still up for a double latte in a single cup?" Not only did they remember my name, they made a point of remembering my strange taste in coffee after 3 months of being away.

They asked if I was busy: my reply was that I would be soon. Not right now, though. Noting this, Steve brought my coffee around to my side of the counter and began to tell me how nasty the storm had been while I was away. "Water up to here. You should have seen it ....."

I'm definitely one of the Family now.

Recently, my coffee obsession reached the stage where I travel with my own small stove-top espresso maker. When I'm in San Francisco, I make a stove-top espresso each morning with breakfast. However, on weekends, I make a point of going and seeing Steve and his team to get my double latte in a single cup, a great greeting, and some news on the coffee shop and the rest of the Family.

# Family to Blindly Proud Grandparents

## Challenges

1. As with the friends to family transition, genuinely exceeding our family's expectations can be quite a challenge, because we've already established this as our modus operandi—now we've really got to "raise the stakes," so that they can take pleasure in being our Customer and become our Blindly Proud Grandparent.

2. Choosing on which of our Customer Family members to spend the extra time, energy, and money to transition to Blindly Proud Grandparents is difficult. This can present a significant challenge, because often the Customers who become Blindly Proud Grandparents have their own unique (and often personal) reasons for giving us boundless love and support.

## Solutions

- Increase their sense of ownership in what we do for them and how we do it, by providing them with opportunities to offer suggestions, and when they come up with a good suggestion, apply three simple sub-steps:

  a. Thank them and tell them that we're going to try their suggestion.

  b. Try their suggestion.

  c. Tell them that we are trying their suggestion.

- Keep them informed and help them feel extra special.

- Give them reasons to be proud of us. When we win an award, refer to our Customers in the publicity and send something to our Family Customers thanking them for helping us get there.

- Be there for them—remember their birthday, and their wife's and children's names.

- Give them time, trust, and more time—make them your priority.

## Customer Transition Examples

This is clearly an incredibly powerful transition and, probably, the most challenging. We're never quite sure what will make a Family Customer a Blindly Proud Grandparent. Sometimes, it's a big thing; however, more often than not, it's a seemingly little thing, and there are as many transitions as there are Customers.

My own personal examples of Blindly Proud Grandparents vary enormously. One Customer that I consider a Blindly Proud Grandparent is a person that I met many years ago, when we were introduced by a mutual friend.

Jim (my now Blindly Proud Grandparent) was then starting out in a new field and didn't have a lot of experience or capital. We talked about my experience in the field, and how I had approached things (both my successes and my challenges). When he left I gave him copies of a few documents that I'd put together to help me now that I was more established (checklists, tender documents, etc). Over the next year or so, I gave him a few more pieces of friendly advice. I wouldn't charge him for my services, because I liked him and he was just starting out.

A couple of years later, I received a phone call that began with, "I've got a big job and I need help." From that time onward, I've worked for and with Jim on many projects. He has sung my praises to more people than I can imagine, introducing me to some key clients with phrases like, "Ken's the best there is." These clients who are now Friends or Family and are referring me to other people, though never quite as passionately and supportively as Jim.

The flip side of developing amazing Blindly Proud Grandparents through longer-term relationships, like Jim, is shown by a Customer of mine in South Africa. In this example, time didn't permit a longer-term relationship to be built, because it was my first visit to South Africa, and I was only there for 2 weeks. And yet, a similar level of trust was developed in a short time because of a series of circumstances—I came highly recommended, this Customer needed exactly what I could provide at exactly the time that I could provide it (he was receptive and I was giving), and we "hit it off" immediately.

This Customer was a Stranger until he attended a half-day workshop of mine. The workshop included some new techniques I'd been developing that struck a cord with him. He immediately successfully applied several of these techniques, and, suddenly, people would meet me at events and say, "Yes, Alan mentioned you; I understand that you're one of the best coaches in the world. Thank you for coming here."

In short, four hours lead to an incredible reputation in one city.

We never know when, or how, we'll create a Blindly Proud Grandparent—my best advice for this transition is to keep applying all of our Customer Service Excellence techniques in every way that we can and to keep being creative by finding new and interesting ways to captivate our customers.

## Chapter 3 Takeaways

1. In the developed world, we value being valued.

2. The degrees of Customer/Company familiarity reflect levels of familiarity we have with the people we encounter in our daily life.

3. It is our goal to help every one of our Customers transition through the levels of familiarity to become family.

### Always Remember:

*Blindly Proud Grandparents are our most valuable resource—they are our mobile, high-credibility marketing department.*

## NOW IT'S YOUR TURN    #3

Who are your strangers?

_____

_____

_____

_____

Who are your acquaintances?

_____

_____

_____

_____

Who are your friends?

_____

_____

_____

_____

Happy About Customer Service?

Who is your family?

_____

_____

_____

_____

What can you do to help strangers evolve into acquaintances?

_____

_____

_____

_____

What can you do to help acquaintances evolve into friends?

_____

_____

_____

_____

What can you do to help friends evolve into family?

_____

_____

_____

_____

Do you have any blindly proud grandparents? If so, how did the relationship evolve?

_____

_____

_____

_____

Now, set yourself a time frame to initiate the actions that you've listed above.

# 4 In the Beginning

For a start: Always be prepared to go back to basics.

Let's look at a few simple questions that you will, undoubtedly, know how to answer; however, occasionally asking ourselves these questions can remind us of things we may have put in the back of our mind, because of the "important" things that we have going on. They may even open our eyes to a few new possibilities.

These are questions that may seem obvious, yet very few companies ask them on a regular basis. In fact, only the very successful ones do.

When they get new answers, they adapt their approaches to suit them, or they re-visit their current approach to see if they can improve on what they already do.

## What is a Customer?

Here are a few well-known quotes, generally attributed to that well-known, universally-renowned expert "Anon," about what constitutes a Customer:

- A Customer is the most important person in this office .... on the phone, in person, by mail or e-mail.

- A Customer is not dependent on us ... we are dependent on them.

- A Customer is not an interruption to our work ... they are the very purpose of it. We are not doing them a favor by serving them ... they are doing us a favor by giving us the opportunity to do so.

- A Customer is not someone to argue or match wits with. Nobody ever wins an argument with a Customer.

- A Customer is a person who brings us their wants. It is our job to handle them profitably for both the customer and ourselves.

## Who are Our Customers?

Basically, everyone that we come into contact with is one of our Customers.

The basic principles of Customer Service are exactly the same as the basic principles of dealing with other people. By adopting the concept that every situation is a type of Customer Service event, life starts to become amazingly simple, because we can start to break our relationships and interactions into simple, predictable categories. For instance:

There are only a handful of Customer categories (five, to be precise). They are the "In" Customers:

1. **In-coming** Customers
2. **In-ternal** Customers
3. **In-verse** Customers
4. **In-terpersonal** Customers
5. **In-You** Customer (YOU)

Try to find someone that doesn't fall into one of those categories. If you can, contact me at **The Centre for Customer Service Excellence** (http://www.c4cse.com), quote this reference in the book, and I'll give you a free telephone coaching session.

Now, let's talk about these in more detail.

## Incoming Customers

These are the Customers with whom we are most familiar. They are the "traditional" Customer—someone who walks into our store or office, telephones us, writes to us, or in some other way contacts us, because they want our services.

Great. We're all clear on In-coming Customers. These are the Customers on whom we concentrate the majority of our effort and rightly so—they're the ones that are closely linked to our bottom line, which is the profitability of our company. And let's face it, that's ultimately why you bought this book—to increase your bottom line.

Never hide from that fact. You want your company to make more money!

Still, you're thinking, there must be more to it...otherwise, why would Ken even mention the other four Customer Categories?

Great Question!

Each of the other Customer categories will help us achieve even higher levels of excellence for our In-coming Customers, which, in turn, will:

- make them happier,

- encourage their loyalty,

- help them buy more from us,

- encourage them to spread the word to other potential Customers, and

- make us happier, because our bottom line will continue to increase.

# Internal Customers

While fairly obvious, they sometimes slip under our radar. These are our team. Everyone within our company—our Customer Service experts, our managers, supervisors, team leaders, or the person right next to you right now (if you're reading this at work!).

How does this help us? By appointing the right people and treating them with the respect that we expect them to have for our In-coming Customers, not only do we have a happy team of people who enjoy working with us, we lead by example, and set the standard that we expect of our people when they deal with our customers.

## Inverse Customers

This one could start you thinking, or, at least, I hope it does. By "in-verse," are we talking upside-down, inside-out, or transposed?

It's sort of "yes" to all of the above.

Our inverse Customers are the people and companies that most people think of as our suppliers, people to whom we are Customers.

So why should we apply the same Customer Service standards to these people as we apply to those who pay us money for our products?

First, we want to know that they will have loyalty to us, that they will treat us well and respect our business. Take, for instance, a situation in which we need something, and we genuinely need it with urgency. If we were "just any Customer" to our suppliers, we'd get the product if and when they were ready to give it to us. (Unless, of course, they've read this book, too!)

On the other hand, if we've spent time and energy fostering a relation-ship with our supplier and we've treated them the way that we treat our highly-valued In-coming Customers, they'll most likely prioritize us. They may even give us (amazement of amazements) a genuine estimate of the product's delivery time, rather than a plucked-out-of-the-air ballpark figure.

Our supplier may even try to apply one of our key concepts: "Set a realistic expectation and then exceed it."

Additionally, by treating our inverse Customers with respect, we're probably going to experience the following:

- Reduced delays
- Better pricing
- Special deals and opportunities

So, why not try it?

## Interpersonal Customers

Now this is where Customer Service can really become interesting—our personal life!

Customer Service doesn't need to stop with monetary gain—why not try to gain emotionally, intellectually, spiritually, and romantically? All of these Customer Service concepts can be applied to our friends, family, acquaintances, and people that we meet on a daily basis.

For example, dealing with others could become much easier if we simply asked ourselves three questions before we talked about making an important decision:

- What do they want?
- What do I want?
- How do I help both of us enjoy getting there?

These are *The Three Prompts*. More of this later.

## (The) In-You Customer

This one is REALLY important!

Never neglect the Customer within yourself. If we do, and don't enjoy what we're doing, none of our other Customers will enjoy dealing with us—so why would they keep coming back?

This rule applies to every category of Customer:

- The people who buy from us.

- The people who work with us and for us.

- The people who supply us.

- Our family and friends.

- Everyone that we come into contact with.

A final question for this section:

## What is Customer Service?

Customer Service means caring, "going the extra mile," being friendly and helpful, not "pushing" or "selling" in an aggressive manner. In a nutshell, it is treating our Customer with the respect that we all desire.

## Chapter 4 Takeaways

Basically, everyone that we meet is a Customer in some way and they fall into five easy to remember "IN" categories:

1. Incoming Customers. These are the people who buy from us.

2. Internal Customers. Our co-workers.

3. Inverse Customers. These are the often—overlooked Customers who consider us their Customers.

4. Interpersonal Customers. These are the Customers who see us when we don't want to be seen. They are often our Customers twenty four hours of every day, through sickness and health.

## Always Remember:

*(The) In-You Customer.*

*Give yourself the care, love, and respect that you deserve. If you don't, you won't be capable of giving it to any of your other Customers.*

```
┌─────────────────────────────┐
│  NOW IT'S YOUR TURN   #4     │
└─────────────────────────────┘
```

Who are your In-coming Customers?

_____

_____

_____

_____

Who are your In-ternal Customers?

_____

_____

_____

_____

Who are your In-verse Customers?

_____

_____

_____

_____

_____

Who are your In-terpersonal Customers?

_____

_____

_____

_____

_____

Now, for the tricky one, tell me who you are?

_____

_____

_____

_____

_____

# 5

# Why Customer Satisfaction Isn't Enough

## 99% Customer Satisfaction—Not Bad?

How would you feel if you (and your company) had a 99% success rate with customers?

Let's Look at Some Numbers.

What does a 99% success rate mean?

For perspective, in the US alone:

- 96 aircraft flying to San Francisco would land at the wrong airport every day.

- 40,000 babies would be given to the wrong parents every year.

- 131,000 telephone calls would be misconnected every minute.

- 7,458,000 people would get lost on the way to the supermarket every day.

No, those figures don't equate specifically to Customer Service; however, they serve as an example of the consequences of a 1% error.

Let's think more realistically about Customer Service and Customer satisfaction. As you already know, I'm an advocate of achieving a lot more than simply "satisfied" Customers. Here's part of my reasoning:

How would you feel about achieving a 95% Customer Satisfaction Rate? It requires a bit of effort, yet it is achievable with the right people in place and an appropriate company culture.

Let's look at what 95% Customer satisfaction could mean when coupled with the consequences of having 5% of our Customers unhappy.

In a recent sample of Customers (from the US, UK and Australia), I found that:

Only 5-6% of unhappy Customers come back to us to complain. That means 95% of unhappy Customers go away and never come back.

The average unhappy Customer tells ten other people and some tell thirty or more people about their experience. What does this mean to us? If we have a 95% satisfaction rate with our Customers and serve an average of sixty Customers each day, three people may go away unhappy and at least one of them could tell between ten and thirty people. Based on these numbers, over a year, between 2400 and 7200 potential Customers could be told that we don't satisfy Customer's needs. If this was the average for every CSR in a company with, say, thirty CSRs, that's upto 216,000 Potential Customers, each year, that could be told that we don't satisfy Customer's needs.

Here is a personal experience to demonstrate the point. I had flown with a specific airline, mainly because several of my US clients preferred to use it; it was the cheapest carrier between Australia and the US at the time. I reached the stage where I had many frequent flyer points and received automatic upgrades and other privileges. However, ultimately I became dissatisfied. Out of twelve consecutive flights, nine had been delayed by more than two hours (two of these by more than twelve hours) and one flight was diverted to Hawaii en route to San Francisco.

This particular flight was the last straw for me, as it commenced with a loud bang on take off, and still we flew over the Pacific, only to end up diverting to Hawaii as a consequence of excessive fuel burn. We were then gradually re-booked onto other flights. To this day, I have not received a verbal apology from anyone that I dealt with, and when I checked my frequent flyer points, I was only credited with a Honolulu-San Francisco flight. According to the airline, my flight from Sydney was cancelled—and yes, it was—however, how do they think I got to Honolulu?

To date, I have told this story—with much more detail including the airline's name—in many of my workshops, so I imagine that this unhappy Customer has told well over 1,000 people that this particular company most definitely didn't satisfy my needs.

However, various studies also show that a happy Customer may tell between six and nine people how happy they are with the Service they receive, and if we consider our Customer Family and Blindly Proud Grandparents, who knows how many people will be told how great we are.

*That's what achieving Customer Service Excellence is all about.*

# The Three Customer Service Prompts

One of the most useful tools that I have found for achieving Customer Service Excellence, along with the five Customer categories (The IN Customers), is The Three Prompts. These are three simple questions that I encourage you to ask yourself before all important interactions:

1. What do they want?
2. What do I want?
3. How do I help both of us ENJOY getting there? (Note: It is a journey.)

The Prompts apply equally well in any environment from a high-level business meeting to dealing with a Customer buying a pair of shoes, through to negotiating with your teenage daughter about using the family car. They lend themselves well to any situation that includes two or more people who want something from each other.

Most of us ask ourselves these questions subconsciously; however, occasionally it helps to consciously ask yourself these questions.

I refer to them as "prompts" because I'd like them to prompt you to action in response to your answers.

# The First Prompt: What Do They Want?

They definitely want our product or service.

It is almost certain that they will also want reassurance. This is usually the first want or need of any Customer. They want reassurance that they have the right company, the right person in the company, the attention they deserve, and the product or service they need.

After they have received our reassurance, a whole new set of wants can develop, and it is how we cater to these psychological needs and desires that can make the difference between Customer Service Satisfaction and Customer Service Excellence.

Let's consider how this Prompt applies to our In-coming Customers:

When someone calls us or walks into our office or store, what do they want?

First, as we just mentioned, they want to be reassured.

Step one - Reassurance - We should be friendly and positive, thank them for calling or coming in, introduce ourselves by name, and use their name (early and often).

We've now made them feel welcome—and we've put ourselves on the line by giving them our name. This immediately reassures them, because they know we wouldn't freely give them our name if we felt they were likely to use it to lodge a complaint.

This only takes a few seconds, which is great, because numerous studies have shown that between five and ten seconds is all we have to win or lose the "first impressions game"!

Reassurance applies to all of our Customer Categories.

Once reassurance is established, we can progress to our Customer's various other needs, wants and desires.

Step two of this prompt will vary slightly dependent upon the Customer Category:

- **In-coming Customers.** They may want to be dealt with quickly, to be given options, to feel in control, to fully explain their feelings or circumstances. The list is as long and varied as our Customer base. It's up to us to determine the most powerful and urgent of their needs and to try to accommodate them as fully as possible, while still selling our product or service and recognizing our Company's needs.

- **Internal Customers.** This can provide leverage in an "I can do this for you if you do this for me" negotiation (although, I trust that you'll say it more subtly than that!) An example from my own work: In my days as a transportation planner, I had a relatively young team member who could have easily found some of our work dull and uninspiring. I knew that one of his ultimate goals was to live and work in the U.S. So, I pitched tasks to him in light of how they would look on his resume, and how that could help him broaden his experience in a manner that would ultimately make him an attractive candidate to an overseas agency, school, or employer. I wasn't manipulating the situation so much as I was finding a way to make these tasks more palatable—and thus, helping him achieve a new perspective.

- **Inverse Customers.** Another way of looking at this is, "How can we help our suppliers help us?" Maybe our Inverse Customers want us to deliver on Tuesday, because they have an adjacent delivery on Tuesday or maybe ......?

- **Interpersonal Customers.** If we don't know what our family, friends, children or spouse want, we're in deep trouble from the very start.

- **The In-You Customer.** Knowing what the inner you really wants can make a significant difference in your life. Without this, it's hard to respond to the Second Prompt.

# The Second Prompt: What Do I Want?

This is the simplest prompt to answer, because it is a personal response based upon the direction of our own individual drives (i.e., do we want to increase our unit sales, our margin, our total sales dollars, or do we want to create solid, reliable, long-term Customer relationships. It's up to you to know where you're coming from and what you want to achieve. If you know that, and you should before you walk in the door and sit down at your desk, then you've already nailed this one.

# The Third Prompt: How Do I Help Both of Us ENJOY Getting There?

This Prompt is such a critical component of the overall Customer experience that the first two prompts will have little impact if not used in conjunction with this one.

Your response to this Prompt will be adapted to each Customer and will include various combinations of the techniques discussed in the next chapter.

This Prompt has two components, the journey and the enjoyment, and if both parties don't enjoy the journey, why should either bother?

Let's consider how these Prompts can be applied to a perfectly normal Customer Service situation.

While I was in college, I drove taxis. It was a wet afternoon, pre-Christmas. I was flagged down by a woman loaded with her Christmas shopping. As I drove her home, we established a rapport. She had been shopping for her three children and had some great presents, though, according to her, she had spent a tad more money than planned.

What did she want? Reassurance that she would get home safe and dry with her children's presents, before they arrived back from school.

What did I want? I wanted to enjoy what I did. My university degree was my focus, and taxi driving was simply a way to make extra money in the meantime.

How did I help both of us enjoy getting there? I reassured her that the timing was fine, I'd been listening to the radio traffic reports and there weren't any delays out there. She was in a festive mood, so I talked with her (as a cabbie you always try to read the "talk" or "don't talk" signals, as soon as possible). Finally, she told me that she lived a few blocks further along, but this was as far as she could afford to travel with me.

Hey, it was Christmas, school was already out, and she'd been a nice passenger. I took her home for free. "Merry Christmas" and her smiling "thank you" was more than enough to pay for the extra minutes.

A Customer calls in with software issues on their computer.

What do they want? Reassurance that we can help them, so immediately we say something like, "Let me help you with that" or "I can definitely help you with that." Even if we can't be certain that we can resolve their issue immediately, ultimately there will be something that we can do.

What do you want? For this example, let's say you want to meet your Customer Service rating metric.

How do I help both of us enjoy getting there? I immediately reassure the Customer (as above). I find some common ground to ensure there is a bond, and at the same time, keep them focused on providing me with the information I need. I keep a friendly, pleasant tone of voice, so the Customer knows they have done the right thing by calling on me and that I enjoy helping them. I smile, use the Customer's name, and stay positive.

It's not too hard for any of us to accomplish this. We just have to be ourselves, enjoy our work, and enjoy dealing with our Customers.

# Chapter 5 - Takeaways

Why isn't satisfaction enough?

1. 95% of unhappy Customers go away and never come back.
2. The average disgruntled Customer tells nine other people.
3. Some disgruntled Customers tell more than twenty other people.

**Always Remember:**

*Use the three Customer Service prompts.*

## NOW IT'S YOUR TURN    #5

What are the implications of unhappy Customers?

_____

_____

_____

_____

Please list three "answers" to the Second Prompt.

_____

_____

_____

_____

What are the key components of the Third Prompt?

_____

_____

_____

_____

Happy About Customer Service?

Chapter 5: Why Customer Satisfaction Isn't Enough

# Customer Service Excellence—a Piece of Cake

Customer Service Excellence can be looked at as a cake.

Let's take a moment to think about cakes.

As with the coffee makers we mentioned earlier, there is a plethora of types of cakes—virtually one for every type of Customer. And even if we all ate only sponge cakes, each of us could still have a unique cake by adding cream or jam, marzipan or sugar icing, wedding type icing, or sloppy sweet fruit flavored icing.

Essentially, basic ingredients might make a basic cake; however, we can work wonders with the right icing & filling.

In this section, we'll discuss various Customer Service tools and techniques that will help us add flavor and variety to our Customer Service cake.

# The Basic Ingredients

This section provides a brief overview of the key ingredients that will make every Customer Service transaction palatable. It is up to us to decide on the proportions to use with each Customer in each unique situation:

- **Active Listening.** Through active listening, we can encourage our Customers, validate them, and clarify their meaning to confirm that we are receiving their message.

  Active listening phrases can include:

  — "Could you please tell me more about that?"

  — "Could you explain that in more detail for me?"

  — "How does that affect you?"

- **Common courtesy.** Never forget the power of a "please" or "thank you." They can go a long way in cementing a Customer relationship—especially, "thank you."

- **Names.** Use ours initially and theirs as frequently as is practical.

- **Open friendly and close positively.** Those first and last moments are always critical. First impressions are the strongest, and we can destroy all of our great work with the wrong close of a transaction. Keep our energy and enthusiasm up at all times and always stay focused on our Customer's needs.

- **Smile.** Always. Before, during and after the call. I know it sounds clichéd; however, people can hear it in our voice as well as see it on our face. Smile genuinely—it'll make us feel good, too.

- **Positive language.** Use words such as, "absolutely," "certainly," "excellent," "perfect," or "yes." Positive language, and the language that we use in general, is so important that the next section of this book ("Mind Your Language") is devoted exclusively to it.

# Adding Icing and Filling

In the list below, is a series of techniques that can be applied to various Customer Service transactions. It is up to us to consider what combinations will really put the icing on the cake for each of our individual Customers:

- **Acknowledge challenges without encouraging.** Acknowledge our Customer's feelings, then immediately refocus the dialogue back to the actual issue and away from the emotion.

- **Allow venting.** Listen. Let people "get things off their chest." People need to be "heard," even if we can't always fully accommodate their challenge.

- **Anticipation.** Listen, as our Customer speaks, and consider the direction they are likely to take the dialogue. This will help us work with our Customer more efficiently by answering some likely questions in advance—that is, by including several key points in one statement.

- **"Because."** Explain our reasoning by using the word "because."

- **Chain questions.** Use questions that relate to the answer our Customer gave (immediately) prior to our response.

- **Common ground.** Assist in creating a rapport find "common ground" with our Customer.

- **Distraction.** Use a physical or verbal "device" to momentarily break Customer's emotional focus long enough to disengage the emotional elements of the dialogue. The distraction technique uses an item that is related to the topic, such as asking our Customer to look at the Web site or a catalog.

When we use this technique, it's also essential to refocus the conversation onto the topic or information that will best help us help our Customer.

- **Empower.** Feel free to give power without relinquishing our own. Let our Customer make informed choices.

- **Exceed customer expectations. ALWAYS.**

- **Expert recommendations versus personal recommendations.** Personalizing a call is always helpful. For example, say, "I use that [product name] and I really like it." Remember, too, that our personal recommendation is often taken as a professional or "expert" recommendation because of our role as a CSR/E for our company.

  To differentiate these recommendations, use phrases like "in my personal opinion" or "in my professional opinion."

- **Listen: Talk ratio.** Our focus on active listening and using questions to prompt customers to provide information can occasionally lead into a situation, where we are talking more than our Customer. In order to help customers feel special, it is essential that they are encouraged to talk and that they feel "heard." To do this, I suggest that we try to maintain a 70:30 listen/talk ratio.

- **Offer alternatives.** Be prepared to offer alternative solutions to our Customer's needs. While we know that the Product X is generally the preferred solution, always listen to our Customer (sometimes price, color, size, or even place of manufacture may be a consideration for them).

- **Plain language.** Don't confuse Customers with acronyms and numbers, when we can use plain English. There's no need to impress our Customers with technical jargon unless they ask us for it, or speak to us with it.

- **Refocus.** If the conversation tends to drift away from the information required to help the Customer, be prepared to refocus the conversation. This is also an important technique to master when dealing with product support inquiries and Customer Service recovery (complaints).

- **Saving face.** Always be prepared to let our Customer "save face"—if they have made a mistake, give them the opportunity for a gracious "out."

- **Silence.** Silence is an extremely powerful tool. It comes in two forms:

*Short Silence,* which allows a count of "one, two" to ensure that we don't interrupt a Customer; this can be applied to most Customer types and situations.

*Long Silence,* which should be used carefully and sparingly. A key time to use this version is when we find a Customer, particularly a "fast talker," who gets into an information loop and doesn't permit us time to provide them with the information they need—or for us to obtain the information that we need—in order to help them.

- **Softeners.** These are words that soften an otherwise "abrupt" statement. For example, rather than saying, "You've made a mistake," try, "I think that you may have misinterpreted … "

- **Summarize.** "Read back" information to re-confirm that we have everything we need to know. In the case of product support calls, this can be subject to a role reversal where we ask our Customer to read back information or instructions that we've provided to them— "a ding and a dong."

When summarizing, we also have the opportunity to reinforce an offer, for example, "That's 3 CS 55 on a 60 day free trial. Would it help you, if we included three handset lifters in that free trial?"

- **Topic timeout/brain break.** If a transaction gets into an information loop, where we and/or they are repeating the same information for the third or fourth time, there is an opportunity to use a "time out" or "brain break" by taking the conversation in a new direction (unlike the distraction technique, which uses a related item or topic). For example, we could try to find common ground on an unrelated topic.

The "time out" should be brief, quickly and clearly refocusing the conversation to the starting point of the information required to accommodate our Customer: "… that's great … May I ask you a couple of quick questions?…"

# Chapter 6 - Takeaways

1. Customer Service Excellence can be looked at a little like baking a cake—basic ingredients will make a basic cake; however, we can work wonders with the right filling and icing.

2. Basic Ingredients:

   — Common courtesy.

   — Names—give our Customers ours and use theirs.

   — Open friendly and close positively.

   — Smile.

   — Positive Language—use it consistently and mean it.

3. Always add a Unique Icing to each individual cake.

## Always Remember:

*Every Customer Service Transaction has its own unique dynamics based on you, your Customer, and all of the baggage that is brought about at that specific moment in time.*

## NOW IT'S YOUR TURN    #6

What are three things you like when you are a Customer?

_____

_____

_____

_____

What are three positive words/phrases that you can use regularly?

_____

_____

_____

_____

How and when can we use a personal recommendation?

_____

_____

_____

_____

Happy About Customer Service?

**What is our preferred listen/talk ratio?**

_____

_____

_____

_____

**When should we exceed our Customers' expectations?**

_____

_____

_____

_____

_____

# 7

# Mind Your Language

Our greatest tool for achieving Customer Service Excellence is language.

Many scientists argue that the use of tools made man "different," leading to man's development, and, ultimately, to mankind's dominance over all other species on Earth. In my opinion, the advent of language was the key catalyst of human development, and we are obliged, or rather, privileged, to be able to use it.

Let me explain my position on the importance of language.

Before language, and even in its rudimentary forms, we could not pass on information. To this day, 40,000-year-old paintings on cave walls tell their story of a brave quest for survival, of the struggle of our ancestors to cope with their daily needs. They tell the story of life, beliefs, and frailties.

While rudimentary, these images are clearly a language. Without a simple language, early man could not have passed on the techniques essential to life, such as the building of the first wheel. Language literally meant that we didn't have to continually "reinvent the wheel." Through language, each generation could grow from the finishing point of the previous. No longer was knowledge lost with the passing on of an individual—either by dying or by simply moving to a new hunting ground.

Eventually, language developed into our current myriad of forms, and the complexity of information conveyed became almost limitless. This is the state of language that we have inherited, and it is our privilege to help our Customers by using it in a positive, helpful manner. It should also be our pleasure, because our knowledge of the power of language (both conscious and subconscious) is the greatest it has ever been.

So let's use it—and use it to it's fullest—to create the best possible Customer experience and, ultimately, make the world a better place!

Okay, you may find that a bit of an exaggeration; however, if we apply the following principles in our daily life, rather than simply while we're helping our Customers, the ramifications can be astounding. I issue you a challenge: apply these principles consistently for a month, then objectively examine the results (and ask your friends and family as well).

While I am saying that the use of the best possible language, which generally refers to positive language, is essential in achieving Customer Service Excellence, I do recognize, as I ask you to, that it may take a while to transition the more cynical members of our existing team to active practitioners, let alone believers. It is essential that they become believers, because Customers have well-tuned detectors that will immediately tell them if the words are only "lip Service."

So, if we need our teams to both adopt and believe in the power of language, it is imperative that our managers and supervisors become believers first.

**Positive words.** This is possibly the easiest step to take to improve our Customers' Experiences through language. Simply replace negative or neutral/non-committal words and phrases like "uh-huh," "okay," and "mhhm" with words like "Absolutely," "Perfect," "Great," "Excellent," and "Definitely." I'm certain that you can think of some more positive words.

**Words with emotional weight.** (The Emotives). In the English language, expletives are well recognized. They are generally words we can place a great deal of emotive value on and emotive expression into. In most cases, their structure is basically a word with three sounds, a central vowel sound, and a "plosive" ending.

This structure allows a great deal of emotive or passionate energy to be transmitted.

Let's try a simple exercise to explore these words.

First, say a couple of common expletives that we all know, though, being well-educated and emotionally-mature people, never use. Say them with as much venom as you like—really sink your teeth and emotions into them.

Now, try to put that same emotive energy into a word with five, six, or even seven sounds.

If you're like most of us, it should have been much easier to sound angry using those short, sharp words rather than the longer ones.

Now, choose a couple of those expletives again. Remember what it felt like to use them with venom (say them again, if you need to), then try using them in a soft romantic or soothing context.

It just doesn't feel right does it?

Try the soft romantic context and the fairy tale with words like "mesmerize," "fascinate," "beautiful," or "absolutely." They should carry the romantic or soothing intent a little easier for you.

The point is that some words work well in one context and others not so well. We've been absorbing this knowledge since we were children and often place psychological value on certain sounds or combinations of sounds.

Within the average vocabulary, there is a number of non-expletive words that exhibit the same composition as expletives (three sounds, a central vowel, and a closing plosive). These words can, and often do, carry emotive weight (consciously or sub-consciously). This category of words includes don't, won't, can't, etc.

**Challenge:** Find a few more words of your own.

Redundant negators and correctives. Scattered through the English language are words that are generally redundant and, depending upon personal experience, carry a negative value. A great example of this is "actually."

*Actually, we often use the word "actually" when it isn't actually needed and, in fact, no word is actually needed. Do you, actually, understand that?*

The negator aspect of words like "actually" is associated with the psychological baggage that our Customers may, unknowingly, attach to it. For example, children are often corrected with this word: "Actually, Johnny, that's a zebra (not a donkey)."

**Welcoming language.** We should put ourselves in our Customer's place. How great is it when someone greets us with a smile and a "Thank you"? How incredible is it when someone "signs off" with another thank you and a heartfelt, "Have a great day"?

As an experiment with one of my clients, we asked the three people closest to the entrance to greet everyone with genuine enthusiasm and energy. These three people (and I love them dearly for trusting me and just "going with it") gave it their all, greeting everyone that came into the office that day with a smile and a cheerful, "Hi, How are you?" and then, "Have a great day."

The experiment spread energy and enthusiasm throughout the office, and soon everyone was smiling and greeting everyone else, especially our Customers. Then, the CEO arrived for his weekly series of meetings. When he met with me, he told me that he didn't know what I'd done, he just knew that he liked it—so much so that he went out to the entrance four times that day, just because it made him feel good. He even called the CFO, met him downstairs and went up the lifts with him to see if it worked with everyone. It did!

Spread our energy and enthusiasm. It's contagious.

**Offer that extra chance to ask a question.** Always remember to ask our Customers if there's anything else we can do for them—there often is.

This isn't just an upsell. How often have you been talking with someone, finished the conversation, hung up, and then thought "Darn … I meant to ask them……"? By simply asking Customers if there's anything else that we can do for them, we could be saving them an extra visit or call, or we could prompt them to ask that question they'd been hesitant about. Let's make it easy for our Customers to find out more information or buy more products from us.

Clearly, the greatest proponent of this method is McDonald's with, "Would you like fries with that?" How many times have you said "yes"? I know that I have.

Additionally, it is essential that both the welcome and our extra chance is genuine and has no trace of "robotics" or sarcasm.

**"Can do" phrases.** Try to say what can be done rather than what cannot be done.

A simple example of this principle is applied throughout this book, where I've suggested things to "Always Remember" rather than things to "never forget."

However, a concurrent rule also applies that will affect the way you use this: We should always respect our Customers and NEVER lie to them.

**Smile.** I say it again, and again—our Customers can hear it in our voice and see it on our face.

I know that we've all heard this hundreds of times before. And there's a reason that we have—IT'S TRUE—so do it!

Be genuine about our smile. It'll help both us and our Customer feel good.

**Make a promise and keep it.** There are no exceptions to this rule!

**Recognize the "proper" nouns.** "Capitalize" everyone who is important to achieving our goals.

Capitalization will helps us achieve Customer Service Excellence through language in several ways. Let's look at the capital "C" on the word Customer, as an example:

Because its use is not the norm, the capital will make the word stand out in any sentence. Consequently, people will notice it. I recommend applying this principle to all of the documents that our company produces (internal and external), so that it will be visible to all five categories of Customer.

This technique to demonstrate importance can be applied to anyone or anything that we consider important enough to warrant it, including our Customer Service Team, our Investors, our Suppliers.

Creating these new Proper Nouns works in several ways:

• The words stand out in documents, which prompts us to think about the word and why it is important.

• Checking and re-checking these documents for capitalization will help us and our team reinforce the importance of these words, because we are prepared to spend the time to ensure that they are consistently capitalized—and time is money, so the mental link is that these words are valuable to our company.

• When our Customers see the capitalization for the first time, they may ask about it, and then we can help bond them with our company by showing them how important they are to us. Once our Customers know the reason for capitalization, every time they read one of your documents they'll be reminded how important they are to us, even if just on a sub-conscious level. It makes people feel special, and if that isn't worth doing, I don't know what is.

I can only take partial credit for applying capitalization to make so-called ordinary nouns "proper nouns." I apply it to words like our Team, Management, and Customer Service Excellence; however, to give credit where credit is due, I learned the basic principle of capitalizing "Customer" from Headsets.com CEO Mike Faith, as one of his basic principles of Customer Love. It's a great concept, and thank you, Mike, for teaching me.

**The "I4U" phrases.** The power of the "I4U" statement should never be underestimated. They include phrases like, "What I can do for you is..." or "What I'd like to do for you is..." A powerful derivation of this statement is a question such as, "Could I help you by...?

The psychological power of these phrases is three-fold:

- They offer our Customer friendly assistance

- They link us and our Customer by placing us side-by-side in a helpful phrase

- They personalize our offer of assistance

**Can I help you...?** We'll help ourselves when we help our Customers, so let's read between the lines and offer to help them; for instance, if the person is clearly time-challenged (read: busy), use phrases like, "Would it help you if I saved you time by..."

These phrases show our Customers that we are attentive enough to have identified more than simply their surface "want" (our product) and found one of their psychological needs. These phrases show that we care.

**Body language?** The assessment of body language is a true art form in itself and can prove extremely beneficial to assessing how successfully our message reaches its intended recipient. Due to the complexity of the interpretation and the tendency of people to latch on to simple pieces of information (and the corresponding tendency that a little knowledge can be dangerous), the best advice is that we should carefully observe our Customers and develop a clear knowledge base of how they behave under different circumstances. Also, it would be very helpful to attend a workshop by a world-recognized body language authority (Alan Pease, for example) or, at the very least, read a good book written by a person of this distinction.

**Be real.** While it is essential that all of these language principles are practiced and personalized until they become part of our everyday life, it is just as essential that we use them genuinely and sincerely, because Customers can and will detect insincerity. And if they do, the damage can be irreparable.

## Chapter 7 Takeaways

1. Positive Words. Try replacing negative or neutral words with words like "absolutely," "perfect," "great," "excellent," and "definitely."

2. Offer an extra chance to ask a question.

3. "Can Do" Phrases. Say what you can do rather than what you cannot.

4. Smile. Always, and without fail.

5. Make a promise and keep it. There are no exceptions to this rule!

6. Recognize Proper Nouns. "Capitalize" everyone who is important to you.

7. The "I4U" Phrases. Phrases such as, "What I can do for you is ......" can work wonders.

8. Be Real. Use these techniques genuinely and sincerely. Customers can—and will—detect insincerity.

## Always Remember:

*To spread your energy and enthusiasm—it's contagious.*

## NOW IT'S YOUR TURN   #7

List five positive words that you can use in most Customer Service transactions.

_____

_____

_____

_____

_____

Write three "I4U" phrases.

_____

_____

_____

Write down a phrase that makes you feel good when you're a Customer.

_____

_____

_____

_____

Can you find a situation where the word "actually" is the only word that can be used and must be used?

_____

_____

_____

_____

_____

Chapter 7: Mind Your Language

# Customer Service Excellence: It's Up to You!

FINALLY—Practice Makes Perfect. (As clichéd as it sounds, it's still great advice.)

Now that we've read through my thoughts on achieving Customer Service Excellence and, hopefully, completed some of the "Now it's Your Turn" exercises, it's your turn again.

Customer Service won't improve without effort. All of the skills, techniques, and tools that we've discussed require practice, so that they will become part of your day-to-day life. Once that happens, everything will start to fall into place.

In summary, the key to improving Customer Loyalty while also attracting new Customers (with minimal capital outlay) is Customer Service Excellence.

The basics for achieving Customer Service Excellence include:

- Always treat your Customers as you like to be treated when you are a Customer.

- Be genuine and sincere.

- Have energy, enthusiasm, and passion for your Customers.

- Remember the Three Prompts.

- Keep your language polite, positive, and friendly.

- Use your Customers' name (and give them yours).

- Always exceed your Customers' expectations.

- Always try to help your Customers transition from one Level of Familiarity to the next, with the aim of making every Customer a Blindly Proud Grandparent.

Now, one last technique for you to think about.

Think about your best Customer:

- Who are they?

- What makes them so special?

- How did they become your best Customers?

- What did you do to help them get there?

Now that you know that, decide on how you are going to make your second best Customer your equal best Customer, AND DO IT!

Once you've succeeded at that, continue it along your line of Customers. Why not make every Customer your best Customer?

And finally: Never give up, because perfection takes time.

## Parting Wise Words

*When product quality is similar, it is Customer Service that tips the scale.* **Michael Smith, Land's End (Clothing)**

*A salesman is one who sells goods that won't come back to Customers who will.* **Anon**

1. *Do it right the first time.*
2. *Fix it, if it fails.*
3. *Remember: There are no third chances.*

**Leonard Berry, Texas A&M University**

*Forget about the sales you hope to make and concentrate on the Service you want to render.* **Harry Bullis, General Mills**

*Make everything as simple as possible, but not simpler.* **Albert Einstein**

*It is not the employer who pays the wages—he only handles the money. It is the product and the Service that pays the wages.* **Henry Ford**

*Men who drive sharp bargains with their Customers, acting as if they will never see them again, will not be mistaken.* **P.T Barnum, Entrepreneur**

# About the Author

Ken Welsh Trained as a City Planner (Chief Strategic Transport Planner, Sydney City, Australia) and Actor/Director. Now he is a Business Voice Coach and Team Building Consultant with LetsTalkCommunication.com (LTC).

With LTC and Australian Corporate Team Building Company, Murder By Design, Ken has worked with over 100 companies to assist them in:

- Developing and improving internal and external communication cultures

- Team and morale building

- Call centre Customer communication techniques

- Staff, management and executive communication training

He currently coaches companies and individuals in:

- US
- Canada
- Mexico
- The UK
- South Africa
- Dubai
- Australia

# Create Thought Leadership for Your Company

Books deliver instant credibility to the author. Having an MBA or Ph.D. is great; however, putting the word "author" in front of your name is similar to using the letters Ph.D. or MBA. You are no long Michael Green, you are "Author Michael Green."

Books give you a platform to stand on. They help you to:

- Demonstrate your thought leadership
- Generate leads

Books deliver increased revenue, particularly indirect revenue:

- A typical consultant will make 3x in indirect revenue for every dollar they make on book sales

Books are better than a business card. They are:

- More powerful than white papers
- An item that makes it to the book shelf vs. the circular file
- The best tschocke you can give at a conference

# Why Wait to Write Your Book?

Check out other companies that have built credibility by writing and publishing a book through Happy About.

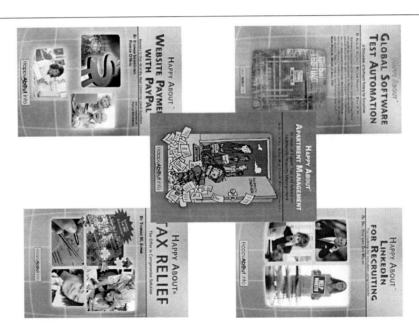

Contact Happy About at 408-257-3000 or go to http://happyabout.info.

# Other Happy About® Books

Purchase these books at Happy About
http://happyabout.info
or at other online and physical bookstores.

## Rule#1: Stop Talking

If you want to be successful, stop talking and start listening. A guide to being successful by practicing the art of listening.

Paperback $16.95
eBook $11.95

RULE #1: STOP TALKING!
A Guide to Listening

by
Linda Eve Diamond

## Projects are MESSY!

From the minute the project begins, all manner of changes, surprises and disasters befall them. Unfortunately, most of these are PREDICTABLE and AVOIDABLE.

Paperback $19.95
eBook $11.95

SCRAPPY PROJECT MANAGEMENT

The 12 Predictable and Avoidable Pitfalls Every Project Faces

KIMBERLY WIEFLING

Happy About Customer Service?

difficult day at a difficult track,
Seca, during a difficult season
with Honda in 1996.

eason with Honda
e yet again losing
d the rubber left
at Brands Hatch.

Neil Tuxworth is no doubt
pestering me yet again,
this time at Laguna Seca in
1995, to ride for Honda
the following year.

and I was second. In some ways that first round summed up the whole season. If the first few races had been held in the dry, Kocinski might not have finished halfway in the final standings. He could have lost his rag and he could have fallen out with his team.

Instead, because he was winning, everything was right with his world. In the dry of the second race, he was back down in seventh while I was second, until my tyre blew out and I had to settle for fourth. Kocinski has always seemed to rely on having the bike set up perfectly, whereas I can ride round any problems. Having said that, when he was riding in GPs for Cagiva in 1994, I thought he was the best rider in the world along with Doohan. Kocinski and the temperamental Scott Russell are probably the only two riders who have ever given me a run for my money in superbikes.

The fact that I trailed Kocinski by just one point after two rounds disguised the problems with my bike. For sure, it was more powerful but I couldn't put that power down on the track effectively enough. Rain also ruined the Misano round, where I picked up a couple of third places while Kocinski won one race and was second in the other. Donington was dry, and proved to be one track where the bike performed well. Slight overtook me with two laps remaining of the first race to steal victory, but I rode well in the second for my first win back on a Ducati. Again, Kocinski couldn't cope in the dry and was tenth and fifth – so I was leading the championship. The next round in Germany provided proof that the year was going to be tough.

When I was at Honda, Corser and Chili's Ducatis always appeared to have the legs on the others. But this year, in the first race at Hockenheim, the two Hondas were in a class of their own. A clutch problem early on meant that I lost their tow and there was no way back. But I managed to hang on in the second race. For some reason, Neil Hodgson was also up in the leading group. On this particular day and in this particular race, his bike was the fastest thing out there.

I clashed with Kocinski early in the race and knocked his fairing bracket off, which prompted him to cry and moan after the race that I should have been disqualified. Slight crashed out at a chicane and, when I had to run wide to avoid him, I lost the tow from Neil for a while. Coming out of the last chicane, though, I had managed to claw my way back into his slipstream and was in the perfect position to pull out alongside. I didn't have enough speed to go past Neil, but I beat him on the brakes at the next corner without any problem. I dived inside, edged him out and won the race. Unknown to me, he'd panicked, lost the plot and ran wide into the loose stuff and finished eighth.

Although I had stretched my championship lead to 24 points, I was in no mood for celebrations. Quite the opposite, in fact. The bike hadn't been good enough to win that race. I had stolen a victory. And, of course, I wasn't afraid to say so. 'I can tell you all now that I'm not going to win the world championship on this bike this year,' I said at the press conference.

So what if it earned me a bollocking from Ducati's top bosses? I wanted some action. I was riding on the edge, yet Neil Hodgson's bike was 10kmph faster. Typically, Virginio did nothing to sort out the problems.

The same issues cropped up again at Monza, Ducati's home track, where the Hondas blew me away. At the last corner, I out-braked them both but still finished third as they flew past me on the finishing straight. This was now really pissing me off. And Kocinski, who wasn't riding all that well at this point of the season, made even more ground in the second race when it rained yet again. I was my usual

Aaron Slight, who has been one of my biggest rivals down the years, on and off the track.

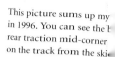

This picture sums up my [...] in 1996. You can see the [...] rear traction mid-corner [...] on the track from the ski[...]

Troy Corser and Akira Yanagawa show their dejection in the press conference after I easily won the second race at Misano in 1999.

Scott Russe[...]
1993 an[...]
rider when[...]

Slick helps me make some
last minute adjustments at
Assen in 1995, on the day I
clinched my second World
Superbike title.

Deep in discussions with
Virginio Ferrari during testing
of the new Ducati 916 at Jerez in
1994. Giancarlo Falappa is
listening in the background.

Davide Tardozzi joins in the
celebrations for my fourth world
title at Hockenheim in 1999.

This picture appeared on the back page of *The Sun* as I correctly predicted the 2-0 score of the first qualifying game between England and Scotland for Euro 2000.

A fan from Burnley shows his loyalty with a tattoo of me in action across the whole of his back. The picture was taken at an event to celebrate my third world title in Blackburn.

I was persuaded to wear this dress on the catwalk of a charity auction in 1998, but it's not really my style!

*Above*: I try to feed Aaronetta, the Vietnamese pot-bellied pig outside our home in Tockholes.

*Below*: Before moving to Tockholes we stayed at my mum and dad's house for four months. This was one of the rare moments when the Great Dane, Bridget, and the Chihuahua, Arai, were not causing trouble.

*Above*: Michaela joins me and Ducati boss Frederico Minoli on the podium at Hockenheim in 1999 to celebrate my fourth world title. Aaron Slight refused to take his position because he thought he had won the race.

*Below*: In action at Kyalami in 2000 before crashing out of the second race.

Concentrating on treating my injured shoulder, hurt during a fall in testing at Valencia, in a break during qualifying at Kyalami in the 2000 season.

I enjoy a glass of champagne with Mick Doohan at the FIM prize giving in Rome after we won our respective world titles in 1994.

I take the mike at the surprise party Michaela organised for me after winning the world championship in 1998.

Those famous Foggy eyes.

Riding an enduro bike in the desert of Bahrain after being invited there by the country's crown prince. I'm not exactly setting a good example, without a helmet or any protective clothing, but I'm having a good time all the same.

cautious self, finishing fourth after a good dice with Jamie Whitham on the Suzuki.

At Laguna Seca, Kocinski's home track, I was as sick as a dog after catching food poisoning from some seafood. On the morning of the race, I had a glucose drip in each arm for energy and popped loads of pills to try and stop the nausea. Considering I also hated the circuit, I rode really well to pull through from the third row of the grid and even overtake Kocinski. And, if I had just ridden a bit more aggressively, I wouldn't have let him slip back into the lead and clinch the win. It was a similar story in the second race, but this time Kocinski had cleared off by the time I made it up into second.

With two laps to go, the effect of the pills wore off and I spewed up in my helmet. Believe me, it's not a pleasant experience as there's not much room in a helmet to throw up. Back in the pit lane, the TV cameras zoomed in on the vomit dripping off my chinstrap. But I had done enough to keep my nose in front of Kocinski by four points, in what had already become a two-horse championship race.

It was at this point that Kocinski started to ride the Honda well. In contrast, my own bike seemed more and more like my Honda from 1996 and we were struggling to find the right tyres. Maybe all bikes were like this now. But there was one difference that I couldn't understand. I was unable to hang as far off the bike as usual to keep it tight into corners. It wasn't until later on in the season that I found out the bike had a new and bigger fuel tank, which was literally cramping my style. Amazingly, nobody had bothered to tell me about the change.

There was also added tension in the air in the usual intense build-up to the races at Brands. Kocinski had labelled the Ducati team 'the Mafia' and I was quoted as calling him a 'freak of nature'. I didn't like the way the guy treated and spoke to people, especially those who were looking after him. The stakes were raised after a couple of run-ins during practice, when he got in my way and was told exactly where to go.

So this was not the place to mess up and we concentrated really hard on setting the bike up properly. It ran well, although I was still struggling for grip, and I was leading the first race when Graeme Ritchie crashed out and was killed. The race had to be re-run and I made a poor start. I had made it back up to third but was really frustrated because Kocinski was holding everyone up. Maybe he still wasn't too confident in the dry. I needed really good drive down the hill to try and threaten him at the next corner.

So I leaned the bike right over – too far over – as I came out of the corner before the slope. The back end came right round and I had almost controlled the slide until the bike 'low sided' me. This is when, instead of flipping the rider off as happens in a high side, the front wheel is lost and the bike dumps you onto the track. I took Simon Crafar with me and Chili missed my hand by a millimetre. My world championship lead had been lost through impatience – and all in front of a crowd of around 80,000.

The situation reminded me of Donington in 1992, where I was desperate to repair the damage of my first race fall. It was threatening to rain, which also threatened my chances, but thankfully the race was started in the dry. I claimed the lead by passing Chili on the inside. He didn't lift his bike far enough up as I came underneath him and he crashed out when his bar touched the back of my bike. But, of course, while I was in the lead, it started to rain. The race was stopped and, after a short practice in the wet, was re-run over aggregate times with Kocinski four seconds behind me.

He was sure to beat me in the restarted wet race, but

he needed to win by more than five seconds. A local wild card, Michael Rutter, cleared off into the lead and, sure enough, Kocinski caught me up and came past me. 'Right, I'm either going to crash out or stay with him,' I said to myself.

It was probably the best race I have run in the wet and I matched him wheel for wheel. The crowd were on their toes, as I lost the front and back wheels in some big slides. Unusually, I even managed to put my knee on the floor, which I very rarely do in the wet as I don't have enough speed or confidence in the corners to lean over that far. Other riders, with longer legs or different styles, do it far more often and tend to get better results in wet conditions. I hung on to Kocinski and crossed the line right behind him, and within four seconds of Rutter, to win the race overall. There were no handshakes on the rostrum!

Even though I had clawed the points' difference back to seven, I had missed out on the chance of two wins. The wet weather had partly been to blame and I could see that things were starting to go Kocinski's way. Riders sense these things. You somehow know when you are going to win a championship, and when you're not. He was improving all the time on the bike and already, I had big doubts about whether this was going to be my year. And that was despite another hard-earned win in Austria. I almost felt as though it was another stolen win, because I was riding on the edge to beat better bikes like the Hondas and Kawasakis – and getting away with it.

But the effort involved made victory taste even sweeter. Another win was on the cards when I led the second race until, you guessed it, spots of rain started to fall. I was caught in two minds: whether to push hard or exercise some caution. But, when Kocinski came past me, the red mist descended.

It was the only time in my racing career when I considered knocking another rider off his bike.

I knew that I could brake harder than he could at the next slow, hairpin corner. He also knew that and, at the next corner, he braked very late. I was later. I should have let go of the brakes and allowed my bike to run through and clip him as he was tipping it over and I was coming underneath. He would have gone down, and I probably wouldn't have fallen. But I hesitated for a fraction of a second and my hand went back on the brake. I ran into the back of him and took myself out while he wobbled, ran through the gravel and stayed on his bike.

It was my fault – I'll admit that. If I had just managed to clip into him, I don't think he would have tried to come back past because he didn't enjoy riding with me like that.

Danielle didn't agree that it was my fault. She had grown to dislike Kocinski as much as I did – and was furious. 'I hate that John Kocinski, he's a horrible man. I want him to crash,' she said. Mind you, she didn't like anyone who beat her daddy.

There was another collision in the next round at Assen – between me and a fly. With just four rounds remaining, and the points still tight, I needed a double win in Holland. I led the first race until the last lap, when Kocinski passed me. But I was confident that I was quicker than he was going into the chicane. 'No problem, just stay behind him,' I thought, just as a massive bluebottle splattered all over my black visor. These things can make a mess, trust me. I couldn't see a thing and there was no way that I would have been able to see the kerbs well enough to re-take him. Having complained all year about the bike, I knew that I would have been laughed out of Holland if I had told anyone – only Slick knew the truth. I couldn't believe it.

My run of eight consecutive race wins at Assen was ended by a bloody fly!

In front of a huge British contingent, I was really down. But Frankie Chili, who was one of the many riders who didn't like Kocinski, came up to me and said, 'Come on! Pull yourself together and beat him in the next race.' I did just that. Slick was told to forget the other riders; I just wanted my board to show the gap between me and Kocinski. He had a bad start, but then the gap starting to come down: +6, +5, +4, +3, +3, +3. It stayed at that margin and Chili hung onto second place. Then it was Kocinski's turn to sulk as he refused to jump on the car that takes the top three around the circuit for a lap of honour. I was really pumped up because I now trailed him by just five points.

The next round was crucial and I told Virginio as much. 'If I don't win both races at Albacete, you can forget the championship,' I said. He seemed more concerned about whether the hospitality truck looked good and clean. I was pushing for changes, and pushing the bike to the limit. But I didn't seem to be getting much response from the team boss.

In Spain I pushed too hard. Yet again I led the race before Kocinski overtook me. There was nothing I could do about it. And, as I tried to stay with him, I lost the front end in a pathetic first gear crash at a slow corner that I was trying to take too quickly. In the second race I was knocked out into the gravel at the start but came back on in last place and had made it up to seventh when the same crash happened again. From being five points behind, I was now 55 points behind. The championship was over.

In my mind, there was no point even travelling to the two final rounds in Japan and Indonesia. I tried to make the most of my injuries from the second crash, hoping that my finger was broken so that I had a good excuse to pull out. I was pissed off, more with the team than myself. I've never been a good loser, especially when I didn't feel that it was my fault. If Davide Tardozzi had been my manager that year, he would have pushed harder to solve the problems with the bike – and I am sure that I would have won the championship.

Predictably Kocinski clinched the championship in the second race at Sugo, after I had finished 13$^{th}$ in the first race and crashed out again in the second, when the bike jumped out of gear. All of a sudden, Aaron Slight had closed the gap to third place to seven points, so there was some incentive for Indonesia. Amazingly, considering the championship was already won, Kocinski prevented him from winning the first race and Slight refused to stand on the rostrum with his team-mate. I watched Kocinski walk into the café at lunchtime, where Slight was sat with a face like thunder. Neil Tuxworth had to calm the situation before Slight stormed off. It was hilarious to watch but, with one race of the season remaining, I was hanging onto second place by just three points. But all I had to do, if I could be bothered, was finish ahead of Slight.

He was never in the race. I had settled for third while Kocinski and Simon Crafar battled it out in front. Then, just as Crafar looked set for his first superbike win before joining GPs, Kocinski tried to pass him at a hideous angle and they both crashed out. I rode through to collect an easy win. It was typical that Kocinski's one bit of bad luck all year had happened in a race that didn't mean anything. Someone up there must have decided, 'You're not having this one as well, mate!' Crafar was slightly injured and, because I had done nothing to earn victory, I gave him the trophy. It wasn't that nice, anyway!

Predictably, I wasn't in the best of moods but we still went for a meal with Neil Hodgson, Jamie Whitham and

Andrea. Following that, there was a big end-of-season party organised at the Hard Rock Cafe in Jakarta, which was about half an hour away in a minibus. Neil was testing the following morning and went back to the hotel after the meal. I also wanted to call it a night. Michaela persuaded me to go to the party, but I didn't even want a drink. Scott Russell was singing on stage and Jamie got up to play the drums. Andrea was on backing vocals, with Aaron Slight's wife, Megan, on the keyboard. They wanted us to join in, but I said, 'Just forget it!'

We left after around 10 minutes and Michaela was furious. So there was a blazing row at the hotel. Sometimes, especially after races, she still doesn't seem to understand that I'm not always in the mood for being around the same people that I've spent the last few days working with. She feels that I should make more of an effort, for her sake, after all the work that she has put in over a weekend.

The fact that I had heard some bad news while out in Indonesia hadn't helped my mood. Towards the end of the season, I had made up my mind that I wanted to stay with Ducati. But I didn't want to spend another season under Virginio. Francis and Patricia Batta, who ran the Alstare team for Fabrizio Pirovano in the 600cc Supersport championship, came up with what seemed like the perfect solution during the round at Assen. They approached me to ride a Ducati for them, as they wanted to get their Corona-sponsored team back into superbikes. It was one of the biggest outfits in the paddock and I had dealt with the Battas before, when they arranged my sponsorship from Diesel clothing. It was very tempting, as a lot of their mechanics had worked with me for Raymond Roche in 1993. What's more, Virginio knew about the approach and didn't seem too bothered. A deal was agreed at Assen, but not signed. It was just as well.

A respected journalist, Alan Cathcart, approached me at Sentul and said, 'Just a word in your ear, Carl. I don't think this Ducati thing with Alstare is going to come off.' The last thing I wanted was yet another long, drawn out wrangle. The Battas weren't in Indonesia so, when we got back to England, I made a few check calls and it was obvious that their plan wouldn't get off the ground. I think they had been unable to strike an agreement with Ducati, especially as Suzuki had come in with a better offer. Even though the Battas were trying to back-pedal out of the Ducati deal, they made one last attempt to try and tempt me to ride a Suzuki. But there was no point in taking that risk.

In any case, I had already signed a new deal with Ducati when it had looked like Corona would be making a substantial contribution. When the Alstare plan fell through, and with it the Corona sponsorship, Ducati were left with the problem of how they were going to afford my new salary of £700,000, which was higher than they were used to paying.

Hoss Elm, of Ducati importers Moto Cinelli, came up with a plan. He was involved in producing a line of 200 Foggy replica bikes for sale at around £20,000 each to the general public. He suggested that the price should be increased by £1,000 so that the extra £200,000 generated could be used to make up the shortfall. His idea worked as the bikes were quickly sold to fans including Douglas Hall, the chairman of Newcastle United, former England striker Les Ferdinand and £11.5 million Lottery winner, Carl Crompton, who lives in Blackpool and has become a friend.

After all the official functions were out of the way, we went on holiday to Mauritius with Alan Pendry and his family. The island was beautiful but we had obviously picked the wrong hotel. It was supposed to be all-inclusive but, when we went to check out at the end of the stay, they wanted an extra £800. Apparently, only the local drinks had been free. I had a right go at the manager and threatened to go to the papers about some rats we had seen near the kitchen and a light that was hanging out of its socket in the swimming pool. He soon reduced our bill to £300.

It was also around this time that rumours started to fly around that I was considering a move into driving cars. Vauxhall had arranged a day's testing at Oulton for their Vauxhall Vectra and asked me to turn up as a publicity stunt, in return for a new car, which I still have. They allowed me out in a Vectra, the car used in their celebrity Vectra Challenge, and I span off about a hundred times.

Then I took John Cleland, the British Touring Car championship driver, out for a spin. He shit himself. After three laps he was shouting, 'Pull in, pull in – you're going too fast.' I hadn't even got warmed up!

There still seem to be a lot of people interested in offering me drives since I retired from bikes. Peugeot have contacted me but, again, they might just be interested in the publicity. I was also only recently offered a deal to drive touring cars in South Africa. It came out of the blue from David Wong, the Singapore businessman who I rode for in Malaysia. I told him that he couldn't afford me. 'We definitely can,' he said. 'We have a very big sponsor.' I have no big plans but, for sure, I would have a go – as long as it didn't cost any of my own money. But, as always, I would have to be in with a chance of winning. And you cannot learn to run before you can walk. However, if there is one sport that you can become good at fairly quickly, it must be car racing.

Back on two wheels, Virginio had already secured his two riders for 1998 in Troy Corser, back from a wasted year in GPs where Davide Tardozzi's Austrian-backed team had gone bust, and Pierfrancesco Chili. Tests were arranged for November, in Albacete and Jerez, to try and solve the year's problems. I had been calling for a return to the 1995 bike and my point was proved when the lap times on that bike were only marginally slower than the 1997 model. I was also the fastest of the three riders and still very much Ducati's number one.

So Ducati had four problems to solve: to stop me running wide at corners, to improve grip at the rear, to make the throttle less aggressive and, oh yes, to find me a team. In the meantime, I had a major problem of my own to solve – my knee was knackered . . .

# CHAPTER FOURTEEN

# *In-fighting*

The problems with my knee can probably be traced back to the Bologna Motor Show of 1996. This is a huge event and includes an annual Supermotard race. The bikes are like motocross with smaller wheels and races are run on dirt-covered roads. At this show the track is set up in the car park in front of a big grandstand, so that the fans can see their road racing heroes trying their hand at a different kind of racing.

It was my duty to show my face at Bologna and compete. At one corner, as I was losing control, I put my leg down to try and stay on the bike. But, as it came round on me, my knee twisted badly, swelled up and caused a lot of pain for a few days.

Nothing much was made of it at the time, because the season had just finished. But, when I tried to play squash or football during the winter, my knee kept collapsing. It was agony. In those days I was doing a lot of motocross riding at a place near Doncaster with Jamie Whitham, Neil Hodgson and Jamie Dobb, a British motocross champion. Whenever I put my foot down in the soft sand, the knee would pop out and twist back in again, making me feel sick.

During the 1997 season, I had a scan, which showed that the cruciate ligament – the ligament which holds the knee together at the back – had snapped in half and was hanging loosely down at the back of the knee socket. I had not realised that I had done so much damage because you don't actually need the cruciate to ride a motorbike. My knee was swelling up after races but not really affecting my performance, so any treatment was put on hold.

The operation, by a South African specialist called Peter Turner at the Droitwich Knee Clinic, had been arranged for after the tests in Spain in early December. Using keyhole surgery, he took part of a hamstring to make a new ligament for my knee, so it's probably not surprising that I now have problems with my hamstrings whenever I sprint – which is not that often – without stretching properly! The whole thing was videoed – I still have a souvenir copy – and he found that the joint was a bit of a mess, especially after the breaks in that leg earlier in my career.

Within 12 hours of the operation they wanted me to put weight on the knee and to try and walk with the aid of crutches. I wasn't so sure this was a bright idea, but I was persuaded into giving it a go. Later on, I asked the surgeon, who had done a fantastic job, how long it would be before I could get back on a bike and he assured me it would only be a few weeks. He must have thought I was going to be riding a Harley-Davidson down the streets of Blackburn, not cramped up on a racing bike.

'Trust us Carl, it's already healing really well,' he said.

'I bloody well hope it is,' I replied anxiously. 'I have to go testing in February and be fit for the start of the season at the end of March.'

The recovery took much longer than I thought, despite receiving expert help from the former physio of Blackburn Rovers Football Club, Mike Pettigrew, who had nursed England football captain Alan Shearer back to fitness following a similar cruciate injury. He took me mountain biking to try and build up the knee and gave me a series of exercises to do when watching the telly, such as lifting up a book on my foot or crouching against the wall. I couldn't be bothered to be honest. I didn't mind the biking, and still enjoy it, but I just didn't have the willpower to do the other stuff without Mike there to push me. 'Have you been doing your exercises?' he would ask. I couldn't lie and his look made it clear that he knew he was wasting his time.

While I was worrying about whether I would be back in action in time for the new season, the press were in a flap over how Ducati would be able to accommodate three riders. It was no big deal to me, as the contract was signed and sealed. The answer came in a phone call from Claudio Domenicali, who runs Ducati's racing operation. 'How would you feel if Davide Tardozzi came back to be your new boss?' he said. I had a big, beaming smile on my face when I replied, 'That's perfect.'

The team, which would be run just for me while Virginio managed Corser and Chili, was to be sponsored by Ducati Performance, which had just bought an after-sales parts company called Gia Co Moto. Ducati were a bit worried that I would feel isolated in my own team and went to great lengths to explain that all three riders would be treated equally. But this was ideal for me. After 1997, I wanted to be on my own. Working with Neil Hodgson had been a waste of time and it was no surprise when he was ditched. For much of the year, the very fact that I had a team-mate had been a distraction.

Typically for Ducati, there was a big last-minute rush to get everything in place for the big team launch in Italy and we had to cut short our holiday in Tenerife. And, even then, the signs weren't good that I was going to be fit as I could barely sit on the bike for the photos.

Before the tests I made the trip down to Buckingham

Palace in February to collect my MBE. The honour was announced in the New Year's list, and although we had been informed in November, we were sworn to secrecy. It was very strict and we were made well aware that the award would not be granted if news leaked out. Only our parents knew anything about it and Michaela had a special MBE cake made for our New Year's Eve party.

I am obviously used to collecting awards, but this was totally different and I felt very honoured. So I even bought a new suit for the trip to London to meet the Queen! You're allowed three guests, so I chose Michaela, my dad and a very proud Danielle, as Claudia was a bit young. I was not nervous, but I was worried that I would cock the presentation up. While I was waiting in line, the guy told me what to do – walk up, stop, turn and bow. My memory is terrible for things like that and I was sure I would turn the wrong way, trip up, butt her and knock her flying! In the event I was dead cool and she asked me what kind of motorcycle racing I did.

'It's circuit racing at places like Donington and Brands Hatch,' I said.

'And do you enjoy it?' she asked.

'Only when I'm winning,' I whispered sheepishly.

She almost grinned – before pushing me away ready for the next one! Then you step back three paces, bow, turn and go.

As I walked back, the video caught me punching the air with relief at not having messed up. It was a great day, but it could be run a lot better. We had to wait in a room for hours without food or drink and then they had the nerve to charge us for the video and photographs!

Meanwhile, Mike had stepped up my exercise programme for the troublesome knee but, when I tried to climb on the bike in Malaysia, the leg still hurt like hell. It wasn't the knee itself, which was now really stable, but lower down in the leg. I was on a new bike, with a new team and a new team manager. That made me very conscious that I might be letting everybody down. But I had to get off the bike after 10 laps. 'I can't ride yet, my leg is just killing me,' I told them.

Davide took me to the *Clinica Mobile*, but they couldn't really help. By the time I got back to the hotel, I was starting to panic and wondering what on earth I was going to do, as we had another test in Australia straight afterwards and only a month or so before the start of the season.

A phone call to Mike eased my fears. 'That doesn't sound too bad,' he said. 'At least it's not your knee that's giving you grief. Try and go through the pain. It's probably because you've not been using your leg properly for such a long time.'

The next day it was still sore during the morning's tests but, after a brief rest and another session in the afternoon, it started to feel okay until the knee started to ache again. This turned out to be just natural tenderness and, after the three days in Australia, I was confident that I was ready to race.

But first I had to pass the medical. They used to be held every five years, which was a bit of a joke, but now the FIM are a bit stricter and have one every year. The World Superbike championship doctors and medical facilities are very good. But that hasn't stopped me cheating the system just about every year. The problem is that I've got a lazy left eye and can only see blurred images out of it. Opticians told me that to try and correct it might actually affect the way I ride a bike. Funnily enough, the brain might adjust differently to braking with two good eyes rather than one. The medical board used to ask you to look at something from six feet six inches with both eyes and I could pass that test easily. Now, when I come to do the new one, I read the letters with my good eye and try to get the doctor talking so that he doesn't see me slip the board down while I remember the next set. It's a lot easier than going through all the hassle of explaining the problem or having to wear contact lenses!

While I was confident in my knee, what didn't fill me with a lot of confidence was the performance of the bike in the final test at Misano. All the problems from the previous year appeared to be still there. This, coupled with the knee problems, meant that motivation was a big problem approaching the first race in Australia. Instead of wanting to prove everybody wrong after missing out on the championship in 1997, I was still feeling sorry for myself. I didn't feel ready for the long hard drag of another season and would have been happy with a top five finish in both races.

That's where Davide's management skills came in. Virginio would have left me alone and let me sort myself out. But Davide, who is a lot like me because he can't keep still for a minute, was forever on my case saying, 'We will win this championship, Carl. I only want one thing from you – the title!'

My initial reaction was, 'I really don't need this', before I realised how badly other people like Davide wanted me to win. It was obvious that his hands-on style was exactly what I needed, because I won the first race at Phillip Island.

The hardest part of the race was trying to keep the bike upright in horrendous gales and my face was bright red as the wind was very hot and dry. I would probably have won the second if I hadn't had to settle for third when my tyre blew. There was no one more shocked than I was to be leading the championship with Noriyuki Haga, a fast but unpredictable Japanese rider. The package was right for him early on, but he did not worry me. He was too erratic to be able to sustain that form.

From the heat of Australia, the next round, at Donington, was freezing, the coldest conditions in which I've ever raced. It meant a real stop-start qualifying and, before Superpole, I was only 14th fastest. This was the first year of Superpole, the controversial way of deciding the starting grid. Each rider has just one lap against the clock. The fastest lap secures pole position for the two races, and so on down the grid. Riders don't like it because, after two days of good qualifying times, anything can happen in that one-off lap which could leave you on the third or fourth row. But at Donington it should have been a godsend for me because it gave me the opportunity of improving on 14th. The top 16 riders set off in descending order of their final qualifying times, so I was third to go. It was a great lap, one that would have left me in the top six, until it started to snow and the whole Superpole was scrapped. That left me on the fourth row for the race and with a mountain to climb.

Although my set-up was poor for the first race, I came through the field to finish a disappointing seventh. After a couple of changes – smaller brake discs and a different rear tyre – the bike felt a bit better in the second race and I had moved up into fourth place before the race was stopped after a couple of crashes. But this time I was on the front row for the restart and managed to cross the finishing line ahead of Corser and Haga.

I had salvaged something from a miserable weekend with an overall position of third for the second race, and 40,000 or so fans went barmy. I even captured the MCN headlines with something like 'Foggy's late, late show'. Even so, the inconsistency was starting to worry me. And it was to be the same for a lot of other riders all season. Edwards, Slight, Haga and even Chili were all fast but inconsistent. Only

Corser looked capable of stringing good results together, but he didn't win many races.

The track at Monza, our next port of call, is one of the fastest circuits and was sure to suit the Hondas. Realistically, the best I could hope for was two third-place finishes. Brake problems in the first race relegated me to sixth but, in the second, I managed to hold onto third going into the final lap when Slight's engine blew up, spewing oil everywhere. My visor was covered in the stuff but I managed to tear off a rip-off, the disposable plastic sheets that cover the visor. Corser was still hanging onto me, but I held the inside line entering the final corner. I braked as late as possible but he braked too late and ran off into the gravel. Second place was a real bonus.

Then, all thoughts of racing were put on hold for a week as we moved into our new house. It was upsetting leaving Chapel's Farm, which had been the first home that we had built together, almost from scratch. But we needed somewhere bigger and more secluded. So Chapel's Farm had been put up for sale in October the previous year and, while we had a few people looking round – including former Wimbledon striker, Dean Holdsworth, who had just been transferred to nearby Bolton Wanderers – there were no takers.

So, with the season approaching, we had decided to take it back off the market and got an architect to draw up plans to alter the back of the property. But, out of the blue, the estate agent rang to say that another couple was interested. They fell for the place, put in an offer and, as always, the estate agent had another property lined up for us. 'It's just what you are looking for – privacy, 10 acres of land and stunning views,' he said.

A viewing was booked straight away, but I had already arranged a cycle ride with Mike and was covered in mud when I met Michaela at the house just outside Mellor, a village on the other side of Blackburn. It didn't make much of a first impression. It was a bit old-fashioned inside because the house had become too big for the owners, a retired couple who only used one part of it. But Michaela loved it. When I visited for a second time, I realised there was scope to make a few alterations. Our offer of £350,000 was accepted before the first round in Australia and we moved in after Monza, the hottest week of the whole summer.

Michaela tried to insist that we should hire professional people for the move. 'There'll be things broken and smashed glass everywhere,' she nagged. But I stood firm because I love jobs like that. We hired a seven-and-a-half-ton truck and, with a trailer on the back of the jeep, moved everything from Tockholes to Mellor ourselves. On the way back to Chapel's Farm for the last load, I was explaining to my mate Howard that the speed cameras on the dual carriageway were never switched on when . . . 'Flash', the bastards got me. I was fined and docked three points for driving a truck at 65mph.

Apart from when I was caught in Scotland, the only other time I have been banned was for two weeks when I was doing 70mph in a 30mph zone in Bolton, a few years earlier. It was the best thing that could have happened to me because it meant I had a clean licence again. But the police were pathetic, hiding behind a bus shelter with a speed gun on a nice wide road with fields on one side and big detached houses on the other. Everyone gets caught there.

The traffic problems didn't end there. Having picked up the final truckload from Tockholes, I headed back to Mellor feeling a little nostalgic. Halfway down the road, our progress was blocked by a car that had rolled onto its roof on a sharp bend. A young girl was trapped but not badly injured. Four fire engines and four police cars turned up mob-handed and the road was blocked for more than an hour, with me impatiently wanting to get into my new home. It only needed a few blokes to roll it back onto its wheels.

When the emergency services turned up, including my cousin Chris who is a fireman, everyone was looking at me as if to say, 'What chaos have you caused here? You must have run her off the road!' 'It was nothing to do with me,' I laughed.

The girl was a fan, apparently, and was pretty chuffed when she found out that she had held up my house move. Michaela wasn't quite so chuffed when I finally turned up at our new home. 'Where the bloody hell have you been?' she snapped. What a welcome!

After a few hot days chopping down trees, starting work on the swimming pool and two extensions, not to mention lighting barbecues, it was back to the small matter of racing superbikes at Albacete. Corser was leading the championship but, already, there wasn't much information being swapped between the two Ducati teams. I had raced against Troy for a few years, but always found him a bit too cool and big-headed. He was the type to brag, 'I've been with this girl and that girl.' That didn't impress me, I just wasn't interested.

I was quicker than both Corser and Chili in practice but, halfway through Superpole, it started to rain. Stupidly, the last eight riders were forced to ride in the wet. Colin Edwards put his finger up to the organisers after his lap, to show his disgust. The whole thing should have been scrapped and the grid sorted out on qualifying times. I didn't know how hard to push and crashed out halfway round the warm-up lap, shaving a load of skin off my toes, almost down to the bone. There was even a small stone lodged in the skin, which had to be dug out and I still have the scars from that. It is one of the most niggling injuries you can have, as the foot never has a chance to heal properly when it's inside a shoe and sock. The first race was also rain-affected and, even for me in the wet, ninth was a bad result. I was pissed off and Davide was even less impressed. Things brightened up when the sun shone for the second race, and I won to pull the gap on Corser back to seven points.

The relief was short-lived. Germany's Nurburgring was the scene of my worst pair of single-day World Superbike results. I was 13th in both races – and it was partly down to bad luck. There was an unofficial practice day on the Wednesday before the races because this was a circuit new to the championship. I had a big crash and landed on my back and backside, when the back end of the bike let go and fired me over on an uphill curving section. At first, there didn't appear to be a problem and I walked away. But, while I was throwing the bike from side to side during qualifying on Saturday, my back just went.

I've always suffered slight problems with my back, but this time I was in absolute agony. And I've always had my doubts whether our race doctors were very good with back injuries. They tried to pull me round and twist the spine, when a couple of hours lying on a hard surface might have been better for it. Injections didn't make it much less painful and, come the rainy race day, when I also had to wear an uncomfortable bigger boot because of my toe injury, I really wanted to be back home in front of the fire.

And the reaction to my results was horrendous. When the crowd invaded the track one guy, who I assumed was English, gave me the wanker sign and another shrugged his shoulders as if to say, 'What's up with you?' Nobody had any idea the pain I was in. Everyone was quick to jump down my throat and the other riders loved it, especially when the press back home had their little digs. Apparently, it was disgraceful for a factory rider to finish so low down. If it had been any other rider, there wouldn't have been a mention. But with me, the expectations are higher.

My back was still hurting for the next round in Italy, so Davide tried to rebuild my battered confidence. 'We just need some consistency. You might be sixth in the championship, but you are not many points behind,' he pointed out. Luckily, the other riders were also still struggling for form and the leader, Corser, hadn't even won a race. A third and fourth place in Misano was not spectacular, but did help to bring back a bit more of that much-needed consistency.

Davide clearly still had faith in me because, during the Misano round, he approached me about an early deal for the following year.

'Look Davide. I think I'm going to quit,' I confessed. 'Unless I start feeling better and start winning regularly again, I'm going to stop at the end of this year.'

'Okay. We'll talk again after Laguna,' he replied.

The next round at Kyalami, in South Africa, another new venue, did little to improve my mood. The results were good, a couple of second places behind Chili. But it was now clear that the two Ducati teams weren't going to be able to work together. The first day of practice was riddled with problems. We expected to go slower in the altitude – but not ninth fastest. I was assured that there had been an oversight with the engine and that everything would be okay on the Saturday. But when I sent Slick round to find out what tyres Corser and Chili had been using, he reported back that they wouldn't give us any information.

There's always been some friction between Virginio and Davide. Virginio has always seen him as a rival to be Ducati's main man. But this was taking it too far. I was blazing mad and spat my dummy out of the pram. 'Right, we're not telling them a fucking thing from now on,' I fumed. Ironically, Chili saved his tyres better in the first race, although I was right up there with him. It was a similar story in the second. But, on the last lap, at the one point of the circuit where I knew I could take him, the low sun made a pass too risky because I couldn't see where I was going properly.

After racing most of the riders ended up in a restaurant called Montego Bay, where a 10-course meal cost around a fiver, due to the weakness of the South African currency. Jamie was back on the scene, riding a Suzuki, which meant that the night was always likely to be lively. Then Corser bought everyone a round of shots, and I don't normally drink shorts. That became the theme for the night and just about everyone was sick. Michaela spewed in our room and Jamie and Andrea were up all night honking their guts up. I didn't sleep well and, the following morning, all I wanted to do was sit round the pool before our evening flight.

Everyone else must have still been pissed because they decided to go on a tour of the area, organised by the Ducati importers based in Johannesburg. The roads to the local lion park were the most hideously bumpy I've ever been on. So, by the time we arrived there, I was desperate to be sick.

The security – or lack of it – at this place was unbelievable. In England, we would have electric fences and automatic gates for the cars. In South Africa, there was a guy with a stick, ready to shoo the lions back into the park! I could hardly stop the car and get out so I ended up sticking my head out of the window and spewing for England. Inside the car there were hysterics, outside the lions looked at me as if to say, 'What's this idiot doing here?'

We moved on from there to a rhino park, where I was sick again. In fact, it wasn't until I woke up in London after the flight home that I could keep any food down.

There was no time to return to Blackburn as the next round in California was the following week. We decided to spend a night in San Francisco and visited Alcatraz, where me and Jamie had our pictures taken behind bars. Michaela and Andrea thought it would have been a good idea to leave us there. They might as well have done for all the success I had at Laguna. I had a nightmare in qualifying and thought to myself, 'What the hell am I doing here? I can't even be bothered winning.' I had no motivation at all and, although I wasn't even interested about getting the best out of the bike, complained to Davide. But he knew I was behaving like a spoilt child and told me so.

'You are wasting my time and the mechanics' time,' he shouted. 'It's not the fucking bike, it's you. If you want to win, you will win. You know that you can win, but only you can sort yourself out.'

It was the first time anyone had spoken to me like that in racing. My dad might have said the odd thing in the past, but he was entitled to because he was my dad. It did the trick and pumped me up. From that moment on, we were far more consistent for the rest of the year.

I had come second in both races at Laguna in 1997 so I told the mechanics to set up the bike exactly as it had been the previous year. In the Sunday morning warm-up, I was a gnat's cock off the fastest time. The only problem now was to move up from the third row of the grid on one of the tightest tracks in the world, where it was notoriously difficult to pass. I managed to work my way up to fourth place, behind Corser and two Kawasakis ridden by Akira Yanagawa and Doug Chandler. There would have been no problem passing those two, until Chandler's bar snapped and he ran into Yanagawa at The Corkscrew, a twisty section with a steep downhill slope.

When I arrived it was like a scene from the Tom Cruise film, *Days of Thunder*, set at Daytona, where he drives into some fog. I couldn't see a thing for the dust and the debris, and just missed someone's wheel on the inside. Another rider crashed behind me but, suddenly, there was daylight again and I was in second place. But by the start of the next lap the red flags were out and the race was stopped.

For the restart I was on the second row of the grid, having been in fifth at the start of the lap before the crash. But it was obviously going to be one of those days for crashes. When it eventually got under way, a rider from the third row came through and clipped Aaron Slight, causing another big pile-up. Slight's ankle was badly injured and Piergiorgio Bontempi broke his arm. The organisers decided to scrap the first race and award half points. There was more bad luck in the second race. Having again reached third behind Corser and Haga from a third row start, my bike cut out and I was hit by Jamie Whitham. He stayed on his bike while I wobbled back to the pits and retired.

But the weekend had taught me a lot for the rest of the year. I left America 33 points behind Corser, with four rounds remaining. I would have to pull my finger out at Brands, Austria and Assen if I was to have a chance of the title. Davide's words were still ringing in my ears and I was determined not to make any more mistakes with the set-up. The only problem was that because the championship was so open, four or five other riders were thinking exactly the same thing.

To some extent, I was robbed of the chance to set the bike up perfectly at Brands through the heaviest rain I've ever seen in Britain, from Saturday night until the early hours of race day. The garages were flooded and the rain left a covering of sandy dirt on the track. It meant that all the hard work we had put into tyre choice during practice went out the window. I rode well to finish fourth but there was no way I could challenge the first three, the two Hondas and Scott Russell, who had all chosen the same tyre – a different one to the Ducatis. We obviously followed their example for the second race and it made a big difference. But, by the time I made it into second place, Corser had a three-second lead. My attempt to pull that back was probably my best piece of riding of the whole year.

The problem that had caused me to lose points at Donington, Monza and Kyalami had returned. The rear wheel was chattering and coming round on me, but only at certain corners. It was horrendous at Brands and I had to ride round the problem to stand any chance of catching Corser. So, just as I tipped the bike into the corners, I opened the gas in an attempt to keep the back wheel down on the Tarmac and limit the chattering.

Jamie was behind me in third and could see exactly what I was doing for the best part of 22 laps out of the 25. It was not enough to win, but the massive 82,000 crowd really appreciated the effort. They loved it even more when I promised to be back the following year because it was the first time, in a trackside interview over the public address, that I had publicly stated that I wouldn't be retiring. I had never said that I wouldn't be racing. But I hadn't said that I would be and the press built up that uncertainty and speculated that it would be my last race there.

My adrenaline was flowing and I celebrated like I had won. First my helmet came off, hurled into row Z of the grandstand. Then I threw my gloves and boots into the stands and was left wandering around in my white socks, which stood out a mile.

Later that evening I was wearing even less. Every year

the track's Thistle Hotel stages a charity bash which most of the riders attend. I wasn't really up for it and was having a few quiet drinks at the bar when the announcer shouted, 'Come on, Foggy, come and join us.' Jamie Whitham, Scott Russell, Aaron Slight, Colin Edwards and Troy Corser had already been dragged up onto the stage. None of us knew what was happening, until one of the organisers threw us some hats and the *Full Monty* music started. The others were happy to strip down to their strides and flash their backsides. But me and Jamie went the whole hog and threw the hats away as well in full view of the audience, before turning round quickly and putting our underpants back on. We weren't the only ones flashing as cameras had started clicking all round the room. I thought, 'Oh no! Where are these photos going to appear tomorrow?'

It wasn't until everything had died down the next day that I started to feel a bit angry about the races. I had done enough to win them both, only to be let down by inconsistency with the bike or tyres yet again. It sounds like more excuses but, up to this point, there had only been two races where the bike had been spot on and when I didn't have other problems like injuries. Those were my two wins in Australia and Albacete. But Davide said, 'You can still win this thing, you know. Corser might have some bad luck and there are a lot of guys around who are capable of beating him.'

Not everyone shared Davide's confidence that I could pull back the 30 points on Corser over three rounds. But I had kept my self-belief and the next two rounds were the key. I needed to beat Corser in both Austrian races, as well as the two at Assen.

To add to the tension within the Ducati camp, there were no clear signals about what was going to happen for the following year. Davide thought he would be running the team and wanted me and Corser as his riders. But even he wasn't sure what was going on. All three riders were in the dark and Virginio also wanted to know where he stood. Ducati were trying to delay the decision until after the Assen round. I couldn't wait that long so I spoke to Claudio Domenicali at the A1 Ring. He was hardly reassuring. 'If you have another offer from another team, all I can say is take it,' he began. 'We are not sure what will happen next year. You have not had a brilliant year, Corser has not been fast and Chili has been inconsistent.'

Bloody hell, talk about telling you straight.

For the first time I realised that there was no loyalty in racing. The Battas had approached me again to join the Alstare Suzuki team and, although I didn't want to leave Ducati, it was tempting to play them off against each other. There have been times when I have planted stories in the motorcycle press, probably more than other riders. I don't know whether it worked, but it couldn't have done me a lot of harm to have Ducati wondering if Suzuki had made me a bigger offer! I've never been dishonest, but answering press questions with a cryptic smile can be just as effective.

Corser was also claiming that the whole situation was distracting him, although Chili didn't seem too bothered. Maybe, being Italian, he knew that he would be looked after. And the Austrian races gave us even more reason to believe that he was getting preferential treatment. Chili's bike was miles quicker than our bikes and, in the first race, he passed me at the second last corner to claim second place behind Slight. But, while my tyres were destroyed, his were like new.

In the second race, after I had altered the suspension, Slight got by on the last lap to leave me in second. I had closed the gap from 34 points to 19, but the other two contenders, Slight and Chili, had also made ground on

Corser, who was blazing mad that his bike was also so much slower than Chili's. I sympathised with him. I didn't trust Virginio and I didn't trust Franco Farne, Chili's engine guy – who also worked in the factory. My suspicion was that he always provided Chili with the best engine.

The in-fighting at Ducati seemed heaven sent for Slight, who could keep chipping away while we took points off each other. And I knew that, if I didn't win at Assen, I wouldn't win the title. Sure enough I led the first race but couldn't shake Chili off my back. On the last lap he pulled out of my slipstream, almost before we got onto the straight. It was all too easy for him. But I felt as though I could get him back until I made a mistake at The Kinks, before the final chicane, and lost the tow. Again my tyre was destroyed and Chili's was like new. I was furious. On the podium Chili was trying to say, 'Don't be like that, someone has got to win.' I felt like telling him to 'Fuck off'.

At the press conference I said, 'I have to go out in front because no one else knows how to lead a race around this track, so everyone follows me.' I was annoyed that I had done all the hard work only for Chili to breeze past.

By the time the second race started, I was still burning mad under my helmet. The red mist was down again. 'There is no way that I am going to lose this race,' I said to myself. 'And I have to get someone between me and Corser.' It was the same story in the second race when me and Chili cleared off in front. I had to stop a repeat performance of the first race because his bike was definitely quicker. So this time, as soon as we came out of The Kinks on the final lap, I shot over to the left-hand side to stop him getting anywhere near my slipstream. At the next left corner he was coming up on the outside but I just let my bike run wide, pushing him right out, and we almost collided. He had no choice but to back off. I had to brake hard to make the next tight right-hander but, because he had eased off, he was not there on the inside, as expected. I was into the straight first.

'Yes, this is mine,' I thought, as I glanced back to check where he was. In fact, I was so concerned about where Chili was that I lost it in the final two corners. At one point I was in second gear, instead of my usual third, and riding erratically in a desperate bid to keep him behind. Chili seized his chance, came past me again but I was confident I could beat him on the brakes when we entered the final chicane. In fact, I was so late on the brakes that my back end was squirming round. And I even banged it into first to slow the bike right up so that I could get into the chicane first. Chili tried to come back on the outside but, having let go of the brakes, he put them on again and lost the front end. I had no idea that he had crashed, flicked my bike to the left, banged it into second gear and the race was mine.

When I looked back, punching and kicking the air, I couldn't see him. He must have been so pissed off at coming second that he shut off his engine immediately, I thought. The 20,000 Brits that had come across on the ferry went mental and invaded the track. I grabbed an English flag to carry round.

It had to be English because I wasn't riding for Scotland, Wales or Northern Ireland. I have nothing against those countries but I'm an Englishman and it annoys me that more English sportsmen don't insist on carrying the Cross of St George instead of the Union Jack. Okay, Michaela wore a Union Jack dress at Brands Hatch the previous year, but that was only because we couldn't find one with the English flag design. We even thought about having one made specially. But, because Geri Halliwell had made them popular, it was easier to get your hands on the one she wore. It really caught on and even the blokes were wearing them at Assen!

As I entered the pit lane, I could see Chili marching towards me, pointing angrily. It was only then that I realised he must have crashed. I had barely come to a stop when he threw a punch at me, which glanced off my visor. 'What the fuck are you doing? I just passed you on the inside,' I yelled at him as everyone rushed over to pull him away. He was pointing in the direction of the corner at which I forced him to run wide.

As far as I'm concerned, it was nothing to do with that incident. The stupid idiot fell off at the last corner and blew his world championship hopes. He needed to blame somebody else. What did he expect, anyway? On the last lap of any race, you always weave about to stop someone coming past. But he wouldn't leave it alone and all hell was breaking loose, so I decided to wind him up even more by filling the pit lane with smoke from a burn-out and giving him the finger. Davide grabbed me before I lost control and told me to walk away. 'This is what we want to happen,' he said. 'It is looking bad on him and good on us if we ignore him.' When someone told me that I was now only six points behind Corser and five and a half behind Slight, I was even more pumped up.

Things had only just started to calm down by the time of the press conference. Slight had already come up to me and asked, 'What's Chili's problem? It was a clean move.' But Virginio had encouraged Chili to stir it all up again.

Chili turned up, halfway through the conference, wearing a tatty blue dressing gown and looking like he had just been dragged through a hedge backwards. It was a long way from the classic stylish Italian look. He sat on the front row and was staring daggers while I told everyone, 'Yes, I just passed him on the inside – a nice clean move to win the race.'

The interviewer then asked, 'Any more questions, ladies and gentlemen?' at which point Chili stood up and said,

'Yes, I have something to say. I would just like to say that what this man, Carl Fogarty, has done here today was a disgrace.' I had heard enough. I stood up and started to walk out, saying, 'Sorry, guys. I'm not staying to listen to this shit.' I had to walk past him to leave the tent and it all kicked off again with people piling in from all angles to separate us. It was all handbags at 30 paces but I was still blazing mad.

So I tried to forget it all by getting pissed out of my head while Jamie's band, The Po Boys, played in the tent at Assen. I managed to block it out, but there was no way this was just going to be forgotten by Ducati.

Their top brass were soon involved and heard Virginio's side of the story, as well as our version. I felt a bit left out of it all back in Blackburn, because Chili was in the factory every day, crying his eyes out. 'I didn't do anything. It was all Carl, he's so dangerous,' he whined. He was also quoted as saying that he would try to knock me off in Japan. Fortunately, Ducati saw sense and it all backfired on the other team. Chili lost his job and Virginio lost control of the team. That might have happened in any case, but they didn't do themselves any favours.

I think Ducati had always felt that they were banging their heads against a brick wall when they tried to get information from Virginio. He was a nice enough guy, but always disorganised. We would often nearly miss flights because he had left things until the last minute. Instead of looking after the important things, he would spend hours making sure that the stickers were in line on the bike. He was weird like that and it would have been interesting to see how he handled Anthony Gobert on a Bimota in the 2000 season, but the team folded because they ran out of money.

I also had a really good relationship with Chili, up until that season anyway. He has since ridden for the Corona

Suzuki team and tries to be a kind of father figure to the riders, speaking up on their behalf on safety matters, money and things like that. In short, he's a typically temperamental and fiery Italian who has fallen out with a lot of sponsors and teams. Even at the start of 1998 we got on well, probably until he became a title rival at Austria – and on a quicker bike. We have buried the hatchet since then but I now keep him at arm's length. It's never a good thing to get too close to another rider, as you need to keep that competitive edge.

And I needed that edge more than ever at Sugo. The trouble was, I also needed to rest and the tension leading up to the final round was affecting my sleep. I had been seeing an osteopath in Blackburn called David Gutteridge because the crash at the Nurburgring had aggravated problems that I had been having with my back. He had already helped me to sleep in the past by telling me there was no point in lying on a hard mattress. This time he suggested I try acupuncture, so I gave it a go although I told him, 'This ain't going to work' after he stuck a load of needles in me. 'Just have a rest on there,' he told me as he left the room. When he came back in, I was still wide awake!

The tension was not being caused by contracts because, by the time we got to Japan, I had been told by Ducati that I would be riding for them the following season, with Corser as my team-mate and Davide as team boss. Although Troy was leading the championship, I didn't see him as the main threat. He had been unconvincing all year and I had beaten him in the previous four races. A lot of people were tipping Slight, mainly because the Honda was on home ground. I knew that all I had to do was concentrate and work hard on the set-up because I was in the best form.

But, after the first half-hour, the three fastest riders were Corser, Slight, Fogarty – in that order. It didn't bother me, though, because Corser always went well in practice but couldn't race. Slight was the one to keep an eye on. The rest of my practice went smoothly and I was confident with the bike and tyre choice. I qualified from Superpole in fifth, which wasn't bad considering there were a few quick local riders. Slight was left with a mountain to climb after only making the third row because starting had always been a problem for him.

After a good night's sleep I was quietly confident but keeping myself to myself. I posted a good time on old tyres in warm-up and then heard, just a few minutes later, that Corser had crashed out. I thought he might have winded himself, at worst. It soon became clear that it was much worse than that. The news from the hospital was that he had damaged his spleen and, luckily, the nearest hospital had the specialist equipment required for the surgery.

Suddenly, with Slight on the third row, the pressure was back on me and I lost all my earlier control and started to fall apart. In the same warm-up session a slow Japanese rider crashed in front of me and I literally ran over his head. Luckily he was okay but it really freaked me out. I became very emotional and, when I heard the 'It's Coming Home' song by the Lightning Seeds, which was playing on the CD in the garage, I started to lose it.

Michaela noticed straight away and went to fetch Jamie, who probably understood me as well as anybody.

'What's up with you?' he asked. 'All you've got to do is keep it together and you've won this.'

'I've run over a guy's head in warm-up,' I blubbered.

'Come on! This isn't like you. You're tougher than this. The only reason you are in this situation is because you are so tough,' he urged.

His words seemed to settle me down but I was still pumped up. As soon as the lights went to green, the tyre gripped hard and I was off to a good start, trailing Haga who was pulling away on his home track. When he crashed out, I was leading and my board told me that Slight was back in fifth. I knew that I needed to break the back of the points difference in this race.

A couple of Japs on Suzukis, Keiichi Kitagawa and Akira Ryo, came past me as my back tyre started to lose grip. 'I can't keep letting these guys come past or the points difference is going to be nothing,' I thought. I dug in deep and managed to hold off Yanagawa to clinch third place.

Slight finished in seventh behind Neil Hodgson and squared up to him on the cooling down lap. He accused Neil of brown-nosing and deliberately trying to help me, forgetting that Neil was still riding for a contract for the following year. Slight had also wound up Neil by confronting him on the second row of the grid before the race and saying, 'If you see my wheel, mate, give me a bit of room.' Neil was really pissed off that somebody he didn't particularly like had asked him to help stop another Englishman winning.

Even if Jamie Whitham was in front of me, I would never dream of asking another rider to do something like that. It probably made Neil doubly determined not to let him pass. And, suddenly, I was leading the championship by two points. All I had to do was finish in front of Slight in the final race of the year.

The wait before the next race was unbearable and I started to lose the plot again. After such an up and down year through injuries, lack of motivation, breakdowns, team fighting and what have you, it was just the same as in 1994. It was all down to the last race. Haga nearly knocked me off at the first corner, which wound me up, and I was pushing hard in second place. The signals told me 'Slight: P4, +1'. He was two places back but only a second behind. Soon those signals turned to 'P5, +2', then 'P5, +3'. I felt comfortable in second place and was closing in on Haga. My tyres were going off, but I felt strong enough to ride round any problem.

But with 10 laps to go the bike started vibrating and juddering like never before. It felt like a chunk had come out of the tyre. 'Please don't do this to me. Not now,' I pleaded. But, still, all I had to do was keep an eye on Slight. And he had lost the plot and was quite a way back. I have never seen the pressure get to anyone like it got to him. So I could afford to slow down and dropped back to fourth. And all the time I was shitting myself – praying that the tyre would not blow at any second.

I accelerated out of the last chicane, changed up to third and thought 'Yes!' Even if the tyre blew, I could have pulled the clutch in and freewheeled over the line. The title was mine.

It felt even more emotional than in 1994. All I could do was come to a stop and slump over the bike and cry my eyes out. I just wanted to be on my own. A couple of British fans came up, including a lad called Josh from British Airways who sometimes gets me an upgrade from business class to first class. They draped a flag over me and started to pat me but I was hardly aware that they were there. I just rode off and left the flag there. Back at the pit lane the priority was to find Michaela again.

The tears hadn't stopped from the moment I passed that chequered flag. To win this championship, after so many problems throughout the season, felt 10 times better than in 1995. People had said I would never be world champion again after 1997. How wrong they were.

# CHAPTER FIFTEEN

# *Recognition*

That third world title sparked my popularity explosion. There were about a hundred fans waiting for us back at Manchester Airport, plus a pack of journalists. It was all very flattering but we had been up until 5am the previous morning in a karaoke bar in Sendai and didn't have any chance to sleep before the coach picked us up to take us to the airport 45 minutes later. I was knackered but that was just the start of a hectic few days of interviews and celebrations.

I was invited to Old Trafford to watch Manchester United a few times, as a guest of the chairman Martin Edwards, who is a nice guy. But that didn't go down well with one person in particular. Before one game, David Beckham's wife, Victoria, or Posh Spice as she is better known, was giving Michaela the evil eye throughout the pre-match meal and during the interval. Even I noticed it, before Michaela said anything, and I don't usually pick up on these things. 'Look, she's staring at you again,' I kept telling her.

I can only think that Posh Spice, who was pregnant, was jealous because Michaela is better looking. Or maybe she didn't like us taking her place at the chairman's table. It made Michaela feel really uncomfortable. Posh Spice still kept up the staring match when Michaela was in the toilets, with all her mates to back her up. Michaela almost turned on her and asked, 'What the hell are you looking at?' But, because we were guests and because Beckham is such a big name at Old Trafford, she didn't make a fuss. Most of the guests there are very friendly. Michaela met Ulrika Jonssen at one game and they got on like a house on fire.

It was only just beginning to dawn on me that all the other sporting stars knew who I was. If I walked past Roy Keane or Ryan Giggs in the corridor they would say, 'All right, Foggy!' Michael Owen is a big fan and nominated me as his most successful sportsman of the 1990s in the magazine *Total Sport*. I was actually chosen as their Sportsman of the Year in the last ever issue of the magazine at the end of 1999.

The likes of Ian Wright, Jamie Redknapp and Les Ferdinand are all really friendly. But it's funny that, living in Blackburn, I didn't bump into Blackburn Rovers players that often. I know and like Kevin Gallacher, who moved to Newcastle, as his kids go to the same school as mine. But I found Chris Sutton a bit rude. He would actually go out of his way to look the other way if he saw me at places like Blackburn's main nightclub, Utopia. It didn't bother me because I don't rate him as a footballer, certainly not worth £10 million anyway.

Mind you, some people might have thought I was a bit rude – including one guy we met at the Stella Artois tennis championships at the Queen's Club in London. There were lots of big stars there, with the likes of Joan Collins wandering around, and this particular bloke turned up on a Ducati with his wife on the back. He was obviously a big fan – and very rich. So I asked him what he did for a living. 'We make furniture,' he replied. We had just moved into our new house in Mellor, so I thought there was a chance of getting some bargains instead of having to wander round somewhere like MFI. I quickly called Michaela over to introduce her to him and help butter him up.

'This guy owns a furniture shop in London,' I said, when Michaela grabbed me by the arm, pulled me to one side and asked: 'Don't you know who he is? That's Viscount Linley.'

At another star-studded event, a charity fashion show staged by a designer clothes shop, Sunday Best, I stole the show. We were sat on the same table as Manchester United football player Phil Neville, the actor who played Billy Corkhill in *Brookside*, John McArdle, and the actress Jane Horrocks. On another table there was a hairdresser from Rawtenstall, called Freddie Cunliffe, who used to cut Michaela's hair. I was auctioning off some clothes with Steve Berry from *Top Gear* and Penny Smith from *GMTV*.

One of the main items of the night was a long dress, but there were no takers. Freddie said he would buy it for £200, as long as I modelled it. I told him there was no deal unless he coughed up £500. I knew I would get the price. Sure enough, Freddie stumped up and I had to go backstage to change. The place erupted when I appeared from behind the curtain. The next morning, pictures of me on the catwalk appeared in the *Daily Star*, and I never lived it down.

Sadly, I would be lying if I said that was my only time in women's clothing. I'm no David Beckham – I don't go around wearing Michaela's knickers, or anything like that. But there was one time when I got caught out. Michaela had ordered a designer bikini and left it lying in the bedroom. I stumbled across it and knew she was alone downstairs. For a laugh, I tried it on and wandered into the kitchen to surprise Michaela. But, by then, one of her friends had popped round for a chat. I'm not sure who was more embarrassed, me or Michaela!

The publicity surrounding that third world title meant

that it was increasingly difficult to go out and relax in public. Utopia wasn't too bad because there is a VIP room, where you're not bothered too much. But that isn't really my scene. Now I'm a lot happier having a few friends round to our house. At least, I can be guaranteed a bit of peace and quiet there.

In pubs it's virtually impossible to escape some kind of hassle. During one evening in Preston, when I was out with a few mates, including Howard Rigby, one idiot came up and slurred, 'Come over and meet my wife.'

'I'm okay here, thanks. I'm talking to my friends, but if you want to bring her over to say hello, then that's fine,' I replied.

'No, no,' he insisted, 'Come over to our table and I'll buy you a drink.'

'No, honestly, I'm fine here.'

Ten minutes later his wife turned up and growled, 'You are a fucking ignorant bastard. I'm going to tell my son to take his photographs of you in his bedroom down when I get home. And you,' she said, turning to Howard, who hadn't said a word, 'you're a right dickhead, 'n all.' I really don't need that.

It has now got to the stage where I feel like I've got something sticking out of my head whenever I leave the house. We took the kids and some of their friends, plus Slick, for a day out in Blackpool recently but I couldn't walk 10 yards without someone wanting an autograph. One of the Golden Mile stalls was selling big fuzzy wigs so I bought a blue one as a disguise. Surely, with my Oakley shades as well, nobody would be able to recognise me. I was kidding myself . . . The first person to walk past stared straight at me. I thought it was because I looked like an idiot until he shouted, 'Oi! That's Carl Fogarty!' I grabbed my wig, threw it on the floor and carried on walking while everyone else was in hysterics. You just can't win. It's great to have the size of following that I have attracted, but there are downsides.

I've been lucky enough to keep a close set of friends over the years and Michaela rounded most of them up for a surprise party just before Christmas in 1998. I knew that something had been organised, but I had no idea how much effort she had put into arranging the night at a hotel down the road called Mytton Fold.

The first clue as to the scale of it all was when a limousine parked up at the bottom of our drive. It was so long that it could hardly get round some of the bends near our house. I was met by a sea of faces that I hadn't seen for ages and everyone clapped me into the room. She had tracked down people like Taste, who I used to work with at Holden's, and John Gibbons, my former mechanic. There were also a lot of television screens and a cameraman from Sky Sports. At first I thought it was being televised live, but it was only being transmitted throughout the hotel.

I was led into the hall, where a stage had been set up and Sky commentator Keith Huewen introduced a spoof *This Is Your Life*. Michaela, and my mum and dad were called up, followed by Jamie Whitham, then Neil Tuxworth. Then they started talking about Davide. 'No, he can't be here,' I thought as, sure enough, he walked in. Michaela had flown him over from Italy and he had just that second arrived.

At the end Keith presented me with the big red book, which contained a few cuttings that my mum had got together, plus a porno mag which said 'This Is Your Wife'. Jamie's band provided the music and Michaela sang a version of Blondie's *Sunday Girl*. She repeated it at the end of the evening, with me on backing vocals. It was a great night.

After Christmas we went on holiday to Disneyland,

Florida as a break before the start of the 1999 season. It was a nightmare – and cold. After two days I wanted to come home. All we seemed to do was walk around, queue up for a ride, then walk to another and queue up again. Even the kids were a bit fed up. I would rather have been on a beach somewhere nice and hot.

Then it was time to start focusing on racing again. My contract had been sorted out within a matter of days of arriving home from Japan. The title win certainly helped, but without the fallback of their income from the replica bikes, I didn't want to make ridiculous demands of Ducati. In fact, I agreed to take a pay cut but with a very good bonus package built in depending on race wins. And my incentive to win another world title was very good. I might well have been able to earn more money elsewhere. But that was never a consideration. At that stage of my career there was no point undoing all the work I had put in with Ducati over the previous couple of years.

If I was in racing just for the money then it might have been an option, although it probably would have taken double Ducati's offer to tempt me away. But all I've ever been bothered about was winning and I didn't want to break up a winning team. If I improved, Davide improved and the rest of the team improved, then the bike would surely be that little bit better and we would walk 1999. When I signed, Ducati were still considering Luca Cadalora as their second rider. Within a month, though, it was announced that Corser would stay. I was glad to have a team-mate again and realised that it had been a mistake to go it alone the previous year. It would have been better to have other people to share information with, especially on the new circuits. And when we hit tyre problems it would have been better to have another person testing different tyres.

All in all, my batteries had been recharged. Motivation was not a problem. In fact, it felt like the start of 1995 all over again. There were still doubters who thought I had been lucky the previous year, but that didn't alter the fact that I had the number one plate back. And I was ready to ram it down their throats that I was the best. The early signs were good. At the first test, in Kyalami, I was fastest on all three days and I broke the lap record. It was such a contrast to the testing and qualifying problems that had plagued us the previous year. And the confidence that I built up made me concentrate even harder. We were quickest again in the Phillip Island test and continued to work well together in the final test of that year's new 996 bike at Misano.

Throughout testing, I had been concentrating on the Superpole format of one fast lap, because the highest I had qualified all year in 1998 was fourth. At the first round, back in Kyalami, I was just pipped by Troy into second place. But the races were the easiest two wins I have ever collected. I controlled both from start to finish and was even pulling away when I was slowing down. The second race was my 50th career win while the first provided a good omen. In my previous three championship-winning years, I had won the first race of each season. I left South Africa thinking, 'Bloody hell. That was easy. This is like 1995 all over again.'

It was also like 1998 all over again that evening, as 10 of us crammed into one car trying to find a South African nightclub. Slick and Noriyuki Haga were crammed into the boot, Haga jabbering away in Japanese and Slick drowning him out in pretend Japanese. It was one of the funniest things I have ever heard.

We never found the club and ended up back at the hotel pool where Michaela was messing around with Neil

Tuxworth, nibbling his nipples as he loves that kind of thing. But he didn't enjoy it when Michaela and Troy's girlfriend Sam bit too hard and he had some explaining to do when he got back home to his girlfriend with a sore nipple. We sneaked off to bed after throwing him in the pool and missed all the commotion when Slick was accused of setting off all the fire extinguishers in and around his room. He got bollocked as usual but it turned out to be some of the Honda mechanics.

After a perfect start to the championship the season became a lot harder from those races onwards. The altitude near Johannesburg makes the bikes slower by around 15 per cent because the lack of oxygen starves the engine. It was the same in Mexico City in 1993 when it seemed like I was riding a moped down the straight. So, maybe, when the machines were back at sea level, mine became harder to control than the others.

But that didn't stop us from dominating the next round at Phillip Island. We were out of sight early on, which had the other teams moaning. It was the usual stuff. The Honda riders, Colin Edwards, but mainly Aaron Slight, spat their dummies and complained that the Ducatis had an advantage. The only thing different from the previous year was that the suspension had been changed a little bit. Even we couldn't understand why we were as much as 18 seconds better than the others. Troy made no mistakes in the first race, on his home track, and beat me. In the second race, I actually crossed the start line in front of him but he had better drive out of the last corner and, in the space of the few yards to the finish line, he won by five thousandths of a second. I've seen the video a few times and I'm still convinced I won!

It was a similar story at Donington. I won the first and was second in the second race. The Honda riders turned up at the pre-race press conference with faces like slapped arses. Perhaps they should have been doing as much work as we were in qualifying. I had blown two tyres in Australia, trying to find the right one. The other riders hadn't put in anywhere near as many laps as we did that weekend. They were in and out all the time and not doing race distances. I said at the time, 'I'm riding better than last year and we are working harder as a team. It's no surprise to me.'

As it turned out, I won the first race at Donington quite comfortably – but it was probably one of the hardest all year. Everyone thought I was cruising, because I kept a three-second lead on Aaron Slight. They didn't realise that it was like riding on marbles as my tyre was completely destroyed and I pushed as hard as I've ever done in the final 10 laps because I wanted to win so badly in England. Slight said afterwards that there was nothing he could do to catch me. 'God man, if only you knew how hard it was to keep you at that distance,' I thought.

That effort took it out of me for the second race. Although we stiffened the suspension, I was always going to be hard pushed to repeat the win. I knew I had the beating of Troy when our tyres lost grip because I was always able to dig down deeper and find the necessary aggression. But there was no way I could compete with Edwards. If he had not had problems in the first race, he would probably have won that.

And, in some ways, I was glad he won the second. At least it would stop their moaning for a couple of weeks. Someone actually had the nerve to come up to me and ask me if I had let Edwards win that race because everyone was whinging about Ducati! I couldn't believe it. 'What do you fucking well think?' I snapped. 'Have I ever let anyone win a race? You're talking to *me* now. If someone offered me a million pounds to forfeit a race, I wouldn't do it.'

The performance of the Honda worried me a bit but I expected to win in Albacete, which has always been one of my stronger tracks. Sure enough, despite more problems with grip coming out of first gear corners, I achieved my first pole position since 1995 in Japan. It had been a standing joke around the paddock. 'He can't go fast in practice, but just wins races and world titles,' they said. As long as I've been on the front row, it hasn't really bothered me. One fast lap doesn't win a race or a world title. Very often I can do 25 fast laps better than just one.

On race day all the Japanese bikes were faster than our machines. In fact, Akira Yanagawa should have won both races on his Kawasaki, but couldn't pass anyone. Considering the problems, a pair of third places in races won by Haga, on a Yamaha, and Edwards, was not too bad for me and my championship lead was extended. Even so, I was disgusted and I had a face like stone on the rostrum. Davide recognised this immediately. 'That's the best I've seen you ride,' he said. 'We just didn't have the package for you to win the race.' Yet commentators and journalists continued to say that the Ducati had good drive coming out of slow corners. It just goes to show that they haven't got a clue what they are talking about. Ducatis are good coming out of third gear corners, but not first. That's where the Japanese bikes are so much better.

While I had been optimistic for Albacete, I didn't have good vibes about Monza. For the previous two years the Hondas had been miles quicker, on a track with long straights. In the past it had been important to be in the right position for a passing manoeuvre on the final lap. But this year our bikes were only a couple of kmph slower than the Hondas, so I wasn't too worried about qualifying on the second row. And, crucially, the start-finish line had been moved from the end of the straight to the exit of the last corner. It was perfect for me. Now the best rider would win and not the rider on the fastest bike, as happened in 1997 when I led out of the corner and was passed by both the Hondas down the straight.

The first race of the 1999 round with Colin Edwards was the highlight of the whole year. He had a slight speed advantage but I was all over him in the chicanes to win. Second time out I was behind Edwards going into the long final corner but gaining all the time. Just as we were exiting the corner, and lifting the bikes up, I timed the move perfectly and caught his slipstream the instant before we hit full power. I pulled wide and he dived inside to open the line up perfectly for me, and I nosed in front by half a wheel to win the race. If the finish line had been in its old position he would have won. It was so close. But I wasn't sure that I had nicked it. The first marshal that I saw put two fingers up to indicate second. 'No! I can't believe it,' I said to myself as I rode gloomily back to the pits. By the time I got round, the Ducati team were yelling, 'You're first!'

'What! I've won the race?' I replied.

'The times showed that you were first,' they insisted.

I started jumping up and down on the bike, as I knew how much it meant to Ducati to win at such an historic circuit in front of a passionate Italian crowd of more than 70,000. We drank until the early hours around the motor-homes, which is what usually happens at Monza. Stephane Chambon, who became the Supersport world champion that year, usually gets on a bike and starts doing one-legged and one-armed wheelie tricks, while other riders do burn-outs. And then I drove back to the hotel pissed out of my head, as nobody seems to bother about drinking and driving out there. It's easy to celebrate after a double win.

But, by the end of that week, racing no longer seemed to hold any importance . . .

# CHAPTER SIXTEEN

# *Hannah*

Nothing that I had seen in all my time in racing could have prepared me for the awful events at my home on the afternoon of Friday, 4 June, 1999. As I've explained, a racer becomes conditioned to deal with death and horrific injury on the track. But when the accident victim is a two-year-old girl, a friend of the family, and the tragedy takes place at your own home, it's impossible to cope in the same way. Hannah Walsh, the daughter of Michaela's dentist friend Louise and her husband Graham, drowned in our swimming pool. It devastated us all.

I was up in the Lake District with a few friends, who had hired a log cabin near Windermere, when it happened. They were all staying for three or four days but I had travelled up that morning to spend a day trail riding with them. We had just got back after an exhausting ride and, while everyone was showering and winding down, I was getting ready to head off home when my mobile went at around 5.30pm. Michaela had been trying to contact me for the best part of an hour. She was desperate. 'Carl, come home as quick as you can. There's been an accident. It's Hannah. She's fallen in the pool and we don't know what's going to happen.'

The phone went dead before I had a chance to respond. But Michaela's words had knocked me sideways. It was serious – there was no mistaking the urgency and panic in her voice.

Having told the others what had happened as best I could, I chucked my bags in the back of the van that I had travelled up in with a mate, Austin Clews, one of the managing directors of a motorbike business called CCM in Blackburn. I had parked my car at a hotel just next to the M6 near Preston but couldn't get a decent reception on my mobile phone until we got off the motorway.

'What's going on? What's happened?' I asked.

'We don't know anything yet,' she said. 'We're waiting to hear from the hospital. Please get home as quick as you can.'

'Is she all right?'

'No. She wasn't breathing when she left here. Louise tried the kiss of life and went to hospital in the ambulance with her,' she replied.

I told Austin what had happened and it was clear that we were both thinking the worst.

When I turned into the drive two police cars were parked at the end nearest the house. I stopped at the other end and ran inside, asking one of the policemen if there had been any news as I sprinted past. Michaela's dad, Alan, had taken the kids to the other side of the house and shut the door. Alan's wife, Pat, and Michaela were in the kitchen and both of them were totally distraught. Danielle, who was seven at the time, was a little bit more aware than the other two – Hannah's brother Matt, who was five, and four-year-old Claudia. They were too young to properly understand what had happened and just wanted to tell me what had gone on.

It appeared that all the kids had been playing inside and outside the house, watching videos in the playroom as well as running in and out of the garden. Michaela and Louise were making tea in the kitchen, which directly overlooks the garden and swimming pool. It was a horrible, rainy day but the doors were open and Hannah must have wandered off on her own. There was a full cover on the pool and, I suppose, one of three things could have happened. Either Hannah perhaps thought she could walk across, or she had lifted up the cover to have a nosey and fell in, or she tripped up on the ledge at the side of the pool and fell straight in. Nobody will ever know exactly what happened.

But when Michaela and Louise realised she wasn't with the others, they frantically tried to find her. Michaela spotted the shape of her body underneath the covering sheet and Louise immediately jumped in, dragged her out and tried to perform the kiss of life while Michaela rang for an ambulance. The wait for news was agonising. After I turned up, everyone just stood around waiting for perhaps an hour, nobody knowing what to say. Then a policewoman received a message on her radio. She came into the room to tell us that Hannah had died.

Michaela almost collapsed and was immediately sick in the toilet. I was in total shock. It just would not sink in. Louise and Graham arrived back from the hospital a couple of hours later. They had both wanted to come back to the scene immediately. There were very few words because everyone was just hugging each other and it was all unbelievably upsetting, even though everyone was still stunned and it hadn't fully sunk in at that point. Michaela didn't sleep at all that night. I eventually drifted off but woke up very early. I didn't know what to do with myself. Michaela spent most of the next morning with Louise, comforting her but also helping with all the formalities and investigations.

I was just trying to occupy my mind and was having a cup of tea outside when a car pulled up the drive. Graham got out but I had no idea what to say to him. He just wanted to come and spend a few minutes where Hannah had spent her last few hours.

I had only just started getting to know Graham, who owns his own steel company, a few weeks before. We had been out for a couple of meals and then started playing a lot of squash and tennis and were getting quite close. This was the type of incident that could either tear a friendship apart, or bring everyone even closer together.

Later that afternoon, I picked Michaela up from Louise's. She was in a terrible state. At one point I asked my mum to come up, because I thought another woman would be able to help her through it better than I could. On the Sunday evening, Michaela and Tracey went to see Hannah at the Chapel of Rest. It was their attempt to be able to remember Hannah as a person, and take away all the images of trying to revive her.

The press were quick to latch on and wanted to make a big issue of it, simply because it happened at my house. If it had been anyone else's house, it would have made a small paragraph. It was an attempt to make it a circus around me. That annoyed me, and really angered Louise and Graham. The coverage seemed to miss the point that a little girl had died in a tragic accident.

One reporter from the local paper, the *Lancashire Evening Telegraph*, turned up at my house during Saturday afternoon, but I told her I didn't want to say anything. They had also started hounding Graham and Louise. It is one thing expecting quotes from me – I'm used to dealing with the press and can look after myself – but what exactly was to be gained by going to the house of parents who had lost their daughter just the day before?

In any case, the police had told us not to say anything and there seemed to be a lot of conflicting advice. Both the local coroner and police had said that it might be possible to keep our names out of the papers. But the press wouldn't let it drop and, after a couple of days, I thought that by continuing to tell them to go away sounded like we had something to hide. It would be better to make a brief statement on behalf of us all.

On Monday morning, I asked Neil Bramwell, the sports editor of the local paper, who I was used to dealing with, to come up to the house so I could explain simply what had happened. He arrived just as the inquest, which we weren't required to attend, had opened. The police liaison woman was still, even at that point, trying to prevent all the names being released, but realistically that was never going to happen.

A Home Office pathologist called Dr William Lawlor carried out a post-mortem examination on Monday. He said that Hannah would have died the instant she entered the pool. He said at the inquest, 'I think the death was due to immersion in water associated with a mechanism which forensic pathologists refer to as dry drowning. The effect is that when water enters the nose and mouth, it causes almost instant unconsciousness and cessation of the heart. Once the heart had stopped it would not have been possible to restart it.'

In other words, there was nothing anyone could have done to bring her round and the coroner recorded a verdict of accidental death.

So try and imagine the horror we all felt when we picked up *The Mirror* newspaper the next morning and discovered their opinion column, 'The Voice of the Mirror', lecturing us all on how to look after children. These were their exact words, under the headline 'Children In Need':

'A child is the most precious of gifts for any parent. A never-ending source of unconditional love and joy. But today every parent in the land should reflect on the fragile nature of that gift. The shocking finding that 90 per cent of kids killed in car smashes die because of ill-fitted safety seats should shake us out of complacency. And the tragic drowning of a tot in the swimming pool of superbike champion Carl Fogarty reinforces the need for vigilance known only too well to all mums and dads. A moment of carelessness or distraction can lead to a lifetime of grief.'

Hannah's death was not down to carelessness or a lack of vigilance. It was an accident. Kids of that age have accidents all the time. Most of the time it is a cut finger or a bump on the head. This time the result was tragedy. You cannot tie a ball and chain around children, and you cannot watch them 24 hours a day. It just doesn't happen. Maybe there are circumstances, perhaps if a young kid has fallen in a canal, when you think, 'What the hell is a young kid doing next to a canal at that age?' Maybe the parents could be blamed in that situation because nobody allows a six- or seven-year-old to play next to a canal.

This was different. Michaela and Louise were 15 or 20 feet away from where she fell in. I wanted to kill the pompous dickhead, sat behind a desk in London, who had tried to link Hannah's death with parents not using seatbelts in cars. It really sickened me and just added to all the hurt and upset, at a time when we could have really done without it.

And if the paper had been *that* concerned about the welfare of children, they might have taken a bit more notice of the court order that was made banning the identification of the other children that were present. Not only that, they were the only paper to publish a picture of the pool itself. To have been in a position to take that picture, the photographer could only have stood in one spot – at the very end of our drive and leaning over the gate. That was an invasion of privacy. Graham and Michaela, in particular, were furious and took the matter up with our lawyers, who thought we had a case. But that would have meant a long and drawn-out legal battle, which would not have changed anything that had happened. It would only have dragged out all the hurting for even longer.

The rest of the coverage was reasonable and, of the tabloids, *The Sun* was probably the most responsible for a change. The local paper had used a picture of our house, taken from the road, which was a bit stupid because I didn't want the world and his father to know where we live for obvious reasons.

The first half of the following week was just a blur. It had hardly occurred to me that I was due to ride the following Sunday at the Nurburgring in Germany. And, by Thursday, I was on my way to the biggest race of my life. I have never felt under as much pressure to win one single race, even when a world title has been at stake. This was not about gaining championship points, it was all about honouring Hannah.

It was my way of showing Graham and Louise that I cared and that I was hurting, in my own way. Everyone else's emotions had been out on display for all to see. I'm not like that. I tend to bottle things up. I suppose it's a typical man thing – you cannot be seen to be weak in these circumstances.

So I arrived in Germany feeling like an emotional pressure cooker. The rest of the Ducati team had obviously heard what had happened and were very concerned. But that didn't alter the fact that I had left Michaela behind in Blackburn and she would be attending the funeral as I started the first practice session on the Friday. The weather was grey and miserable, which was exactly how I felt, but I just tried to stay focused. And I managed to stay with the pace of the first timed session and clocked the fourth fastest time as we experimented with different gearboxes.

Michaela flew out in time for Saturday's qualifying and it was a relief to be with someone who was going through the same emotional turmoil that I was. She knew, though, that she had to behave normally so that I could try and approach the race in the usual way. That helped her as well. There was little point telling me about the funeral because I knew how horrible it must have been. But she did repeat something that Graham had told me before I left for Germany. He said, quite simply, 'Go out and win it for Hannah.'

That was easier said than done. I had never won at the Nurburgring before and had a disaster the previous year when I was 13th in both races. The odds seemed to be totally stacked against me and, on top of that, the weather forecast was awful. But, after the final timed session on Saturday afternoon, I was confident with the bike set-up although I wasn't producing anything special in the way of times and was only sixth fastest.

There were five riders to go after me in Superpole but my lap was inspired and no one was ever going to come anywhere near it. I set a new Nurburgring lap record for World Superbikes with a time of 1 minute 38.843 seconds, almost a full half a second faster than Colin Edwards in second place. It was one of the most incredible laps I had ever ridden for Superpole. I was quoted in *The Sun* saying that I had felt Hannah looking down on me and pushing me to better things. I didn't say anything like that but, all the same, this didn't feel like just any other meeting.

Religion, and life after death, are difficult subjects for me. I've never really gone to church but I do say a small prayer out loud before races – to whoever might be listening up there. It will only be a quick, 'Please help me through this one' or, 'I think I might need your help today' or just, 'Take care of me'. It would be a bit cheeky to ask for help in winning the race, as I haven't really put enough into religion to ask for that much out of it. But I guess I must believe in something. And I don't want to sound like Glenn Hoddle but I think there must be some form of life after death. Maybe, as soon as you die, you might come out as a baby somewhere else. I hope that's the case because otherwise it will be a bloody long time doing nothing. Surely it can't just be, 'Full stop, that's it'. There must be more to it all than that.

Come race day at the Nurburgring, I was desperate to just get out there and win the race. I'm intense enough during preparation for races in normal circumstances but, on that Sunday morning, I was in a world of my own.

And this was definitely one of those times, as I waited for the green light to signal the start of race one, when I asked for a little bit of divine intervention. I didn't have the best of starts and slipped into third place and I began to think there was no way I would be able to pass Chili and Edwards in front of me. I was not losing any ground to them, but I wasn't gaining either. But an early crash in the race had deposited oil at the bottom of the track and they both ran off into the gravel at that corner, leaving me back in the lead.

Five riders in total slid off at the same spot and there were official complaints about the standard of marshalling because no flags were shown warning riders of the oil. Even Davide got involved, storming up to race control and demanding an early finish to the race. All he was bothered about was the safety of the riders – he didn't care whether a Kawasaki, Suzuki or a scooter won the race.

To a large extent, I blamed the riders themselves. I can't

remember seeing any yellow flags but I was aware that riders were crashing at the same spot. So I was careful to take a tighter line, avoiding the spill. Other riders could and should have done the same. During all this commotion, I was way out in front with a five-second lead. But, if the race had been stopped early, not enough laps had been completed for me to secure the points. Edwards slammed the marshalling as 'amateurish and stupid'. It was appalling in some ways because, as I approached back marker Lothar Kraus, the marshals didn't show any blue flags to warn him so that he could move out of the way and let me through. And there was no way I was going to let him hold me up, so I decided to try and dive straight past him. We touched and he crashed out, but that was to be the last scare. I coasted home to win by more than seven seconds, with Slight in second and Corser in third.

The chequered flag usually triggers a whole load of emotions – relief, elation and exhilaration. This time it meant none of those. I buried my head into my bike, skipped the lap of honour and made straight for the pit lane. The greeting there was subdued and, as usual, the first hug was saved for Michaela. She was already weeping and, at that moment, the whole range of that week's events and feelings just erupted in a flood of my own tears. I was overcome by the feeling of pride and relief that I had done something for Graham and Louise and, more importantly, had honoured Hannah's memory.

In some ways, it was like a winning a world championship. Because to win this one race was a goal that had been eating away at me for what seemed like ages. It was difficult to find the right words to try and explain to the world's press exactly what the race had meant to me, and my family.

'This was the most important race of my life,' I told them. 'I had to win that race, no matter what, for somebody who is not with us any more. I wanted to win for little Hannah, who lost her life in tragic circumstances. I wanted to win for her at all costs. Her dad asked me to win the race for her.'

I didn't really want to take my place on the podium. It somehow didn't feel right but, in a way, I had to try to get back to normality. This wasn't an easy thing to do, especially on such a weird day. It always used to be a tradition in motorsport that the race winner was handed a laurel wreath, but that hardly ever happens now. But, at this meeting, the organisers had decided to restore that custom and I was presented with a huge garland, sprayed in gold paint. God Save The Queen was played and the Italian national anthem for the winning manufacturer.

I didn't have to explain to Troy, who was stood next to me on the left of the rostrum after finishing third, not to spray the champagne as a mark of respect. And I didn't think that I needed to tell Slight, on the right. I thought wrong and the idiot started to douse the crowd below. It made me hate the man even more.

The break between races was strange. It had probably been the worst week of my life and I felt exhausted. My energy had all been channeled into the first race. It wouldn't have been okay to come second in the first race and win the second. I had to win that first race directly after her death. Even a double win wouldn't have meant double the tribute to her memory, as all that had been sorted in race one.

To be honest, I really didn't care whether I won race two or not. It seemed like the meeting was over and that I had done all that was required of me. Yet I found myself winning comfortably again, by more than three seconds.

Then, with just five laps remaining, I slid off into the dirt at a totally harmless corner. Maybe the choice of tyre for the second race had been too soft, but it still shouldn't have happened. I managed to keep the engine going and, with the help of a marshal, rejoined the race but the leading pack were long gone and I had to settle for 15th place and one point. Many other riders would have thrown in the towel and not bothered to get back into the race. So, in that respect, I suppose my competitive instincts were intact after the draining events of the morning. But it was a fall that bugged me for the rest of the season. It was impossible not to think that, had I lost the championship by anything less than 24 points, it would have been due to that one stupid error that was totally out of character.

Within 20 minutes of the second race finishing I was dashing to the airport to catch an 8.30pm flight home. It was a meeting I was glad to see the back of, a weird weekend in every respect – when something or someone seemed to be controlling what was happening. The poor weather had held off and any obstacle that seemed to be in my way during the first race just seemed to disappear. When Chili and Edwards rode into the gravel, it seemed as though someone was saying, 'There's your clear track, Carl, go and do what you have to do.' Then there was the crash in race two. That appeared to say, 'We let you win the first race for Hannah; this is pay back time.'

It was also odd that the Nurburgring officials had decided to give podium finishers a garland, instead of the usual flowers. This was something I could give to Louise and Graham as a lasting tribute to Hannah and it has now been mounted in a gold frame, with a picture of her in the middle.

Graham and Louise had already decided, before the accident, to come and watch me in the next round at Misano. I suppose this was a make or break time for our friendship and it must not have been easy for them to see it through.

Everybody was coming to terms with it in their own way. I had my racing to keep me focused and the Nurburgring experience had brought a lot of my deeper feelings to the surface. The fact that I had seen tragedies throughout my racing career also helped me to cope better than the others. But I found this very hard to deal with because it wasn't an adult, who was totally aware of the dangers of his sport, who had died. It was a beautiful little girl. Graham also threw himself into his work. But Louise and Michaela had been present and had to live with the images. It will stay with them much more vividly, and it was good for them to spend time together after the tragedy and talk it through.

I had actually flown out to Italy the week before the meeting for an aborted testing session at Misano. In the event, the track was in no condition for proper testing, so I took advantage of some spare time to visit Davide's home and we had our first chat about a contract for the following year.

I had also spent a couple of days trail riding around the mountains of Bologna with Slick and a few of the other Ducati lads. Two mechanics ended up in hospital with a broken thumb and badly sprained wrist, after falling off their bikes. I was staying in Cattolica, a resort on the Adriatic coast about 10 minutes drive (Italian-style) from the track and was already pretty chilled out by the time Michaela, Louise and the kids arrived on the Sunday before the San Marino round. Graham had work commitments and joined us on the Wednesday.

We were all able to spend a lot of time together, just messing around on the beach during the day and enjoying the best Italian food and wine at night. Louise and Graham were naturally still grieving – deeply – but there were signs as the week wore on that the break was doing them some good. Sure, there were difficult moments that anyone who has experienced this kind of thing has to work through. For instance, it was strange watching their son Matt and the other kids climb into the hotel pool for the first time. I'm sure that Graham and Louise didn't want to take their eyes off them for a second.

Nobody had really known what to do about the swimming pool at home after the accident. Michaela has not been back in to this day and I wanted Graham's advice before I used it. 'What do you want me to do with that thing?' I asked, pointing to the pool. 'Do you want me to fill it in?' He told me to leave it as it was and I think that was the right decision. If we had filled it in visitors would always have asked 'What used to be there?' And then we would have had to go through the painful story.

Misano is not one of my favourite tracks and, going into that meeting, I had never won there. But I was unusually relaxed and I tend to feel pretty much at home in Italy, anyway. Graham and Louise spent a lot of time around the Ducati hospitality compound, which becomes almost home for a few days. And it didn't harm everyone's mood when I won both races. Misano was probably Corser's best track and it niggled him when I won Superpole.

I wanted to try the hardest tyre that Michelin had available. Michelin warned that it was too hard and too cold and Luca Gasbarro, who is effectively my chief mechanic, said, 'No, Carl, you're not using it. It's too cold and dangerous.'

'Put it in,' I insisted. 'Don't say another word, just put the tyre in.'

When it came to warm-up I was a bit nervous because I was out on a limb. But I was the quickest out there without even trying and the tyre looked perfect. I was way out in front in the first race but ended up just managing to fend off Troy because I had a gear selector problem, which was costing me time. People said that he had conserved his tyres better. That was bullshit. Riders don't conserve tyres – they ride as hard as they can for 25 laps. There were no such worries in the second race, which I won by miles. My friend Geoff, who owns a helicopter business, and his girlfriend, Mandy, had also flown out for the races and, by Sunday night, everyone seemed pretty relaxed. It was clear that, if anything, our friendship with Louise and Graham was even stronger.

It seemed, at that stage, that the kids had been pretty unaffected. They are probably at the best age to deal with something like this, when they don't really understand what's happened. Graham has two children from a previous marriage and his 10-year-old took things really badly. Matt didn't seem to mention the accident much at first and his mum and dad made a deliberate attempt to keep him occupied by maybe being a bit more lenient than usual. But he went through a bit of a bad patch later on. We have explained to our two what happened and they don't seem to have been too upset, although Danielle was concerned at first and wrote notes to Graham and Louise saying how sorry she was.

The next difficult time was the day Hannah would have been three. I think everyone wanted some kind of lasting memorial, so we decided to club together and buy some play equipment for the nursery she had attended. It wasn't meant to be a morbid occasion, although there were obviously a few tears when the equipment was handed over. It was our way of helping to keep Hannah's memory alive. Everybody has their own way of doing that. For instance, there is a picture of her on our kitchen cabinet, which Michaela wanted. Louise also has photos of Hannah all over the house. While it's impossible to say how you would react unless the same thing happened to you, I would probably have been inclined to take all the pictures down. I would find it too upsetting.

Time is the only real healer, though. I guess the first 12 months are probably the worst and then it might start to become a bit easier to live with. It is not something that will ever be forgotten – and we all wish we could turn back the clock.

# CHAPTER SEVENTEEN

# *King Carl*

Michael Doohan was on the same flight from London to San Francisco for the next round at Laguna Seca. He was going to see a specialist about the injuries from that big crash in Spain, which ended his career. He ran wide coming out of a corner and was heading for another left-hander when he clipped a white line, which was wet following early morning rain, and crashed at about 120mph. He suffered bad muscle and nerve damage to a wrist, badly damaged his knee ligaments and broke a collarbone.

Doohan looked terrible. 'He's never going to race again,' I thought. But he was very interested to hear about what was happening in superbikes and my plans for the following year.

'I might be running a team in Grands Prix. Would you be interested?' he asked.

'I don't know, Mick, I think I'm too old for that.'

'Bollocks man, it's not like it used to be. You could make the switch without a problem. The bikes are so much easier to ride nowadays,' he said.

I think that pissed him off a bit. He had mastered the bikes when they were difficult and won five world titles. When the fuel was changed to unleaded, people like Max Biaggi had just jumped on a 500cc and won straight away. Loris Capirossi and Valentino Rossi made the move from

250ccs and were among the fastest in testing straight away. I'm sick of these old pro-GP journalists saying that the 500s are so hard to ride. They should listen to Doohan, the man himself.

We helped Doohan with his bags at San Francisco airport and made sure he was okay getting into his hire car. As we drove down to Laguna, I asked Michaela what she thought about what Doohan had been saying. She said, 'Let's not go through all that again. It's nice and simple now and you've not got many years left.'

I had given Doohan the impression that I wasn't too interested, and that was how it was left. If the same thing had happened five years before then I would have pushed it all the way. But I can't help thinking that I would have been more motivated for the 2000 season if I was going into 500s.

I was glad to be taking a 55-point lead into the Laguna races as it's not a circuit where a rider like me can carry a lot of corner speed. If you tried to run fast through the first three corners, you would lose the front end. So I had to brake hard, then slide into bends like some of the other guys do, but that's not really my style. And I've always struggled in qualifying at that track. Putting a new rear tyre in didn't really make any difference, as it usually did, because I was always pushing the front tyre.

Where everyone else gains that extra half a second or more with a new tyre, I recorded the same times. That's why I was on the third row of the grid for the fifth year in succession. Still, by the end of the first lap, I was in front of Troy, who had been on pole. He claimed that a few people had cheated at the start. Although I finished fifth it was a moral victory as my nearest rivals, Troy and Edwards, were sixth and fourth respectively. It was the only time all year when we all had tyre problems at the same time. Troy gambled on a different tyre for the second race, which worked because he was second while I swapped fourth and fifth with Edwards. But, overall, I had only lost a couple of points in the championship, which was as good as I could have hoped for.

Next stop, Brands! The build-up to the race was incredible. Almost every national newspaper did a full feature on me. I think it helped that Britain wasn't having any success in any other sport. Geoff flew me down to the Brands Hatch Thistle Hotel on the Wednesday before the race, and we flew into London on the Thursday for the big press conference and photoshoot in Trafalgar Square. I felt sorry for the other riders. It was as though they didn't exist in the eyes of the media. Not a single picture of them appeared anywhere.

While I was confident that we could win there, it was obvious during Friday's qualifying that we were struggling. Nothing that we tried seemed to be working. The pressure might have been starting to show because I was desperate to find the right set-up. When I tried to do a race distance on the Saturday, Davide pulled me in because my times were too slow. The tyre didn't seem to be the problem because I had noted that it looked good. I thought the slow times were being caused by the set-up. But I was told that they wanted to try a different tyre, which had helped Troy achieve better times.

By Superpole, I was still not confident that we knew what we wanted for the race. But a brief shower meant that Superpole was scrapped and riders were given 12 laps in which to set their fastest time. Davide had sensed we were struggling, and that the expectations were perhaps getting to me. So he grabbed me by the visor to shake me up. 'Just go out and ride,' he growled. My lap, in front of a massive 30,000 crowd who had turned up to watch qualifying, matched the one I had ridden at the Nurburgring – I was hanging off everywhere, on the limit at every corner. It was going to take something extra-special to wrestle pole position from me and no one came anywhere near it.

The hotel at the track had been too busy the previous couple of nights, so I decided to stay in the motorhome that we had rented. There were 100,000 people expected – although, come the day, it was more like 120,000 – and I didn't want to wrestle my way through the crowds first thing in the morning. But, because it wasn't my motorhome, I couldn't relax. There was no television to watch and nothing to make a brew with. It was all a bit of a cock-up and I had a rough night's sleep.

There was an important decision to make first thing the next morning. The team wanted me to continue to use the harder 'P' tyre compound that Troy had chosen. I wasn't so sure and I should have stuck with my instincts, as I had at Misano, and opted for a softer 'M'. I had a great start but didn't really want to be in front early on. Edwards came past and I sat in behind him for three or four laps. 'There's not a problem here. This is very comfortable,' I thought. After 10 laps he was starting to pull away, because I was losing grip and running wide. Troy appeared to be having the same problems but, when I was back down in fourth place, my bike started to judder and bang. 'How the hell am I going to bring this thing home?' I asked myself, just as there was a loud bang at Dingle Dell. A huge chunk had flown out of the tyre and I went straight into the pits.

With a quick change I might have been able to salvage a few points in the lower positions. But the pit stop was a joke. It was like Laurel and Hardy. First the stand snapped on the welding. Then they couldn't get the wheel nut off, then the spanner. All I could do was stand by in embarrass-ment. When I rejoined the race I was a lap behind and out of the points. I have never been so gutted and livid. Why did this have to happen in front of an incredible crowd of 120,000 of my fans?

When I discovered that Honda had used the same tyre to come first and second, I was really stumped. But we opted to use a 16.5in, instead of the 17in, as that would run cooler. We also tried a new compound, which Michelin promised would not fall apart, although they weren't sure what the grip would be like. We changed our minds so many times between races but decided on the safe option. John Reynolds had used the same tyre in the first race to finish fourth, so I didn't think we could go too far wrong.

It was the worst tyre I have ever put on in my career. I was even sliding around on the warm-up lap. It just about got me through to the end of the race before it also blew on the last lap. I had to ride around the problem from the word go and I manhandled the bike into fourth place, which was a great result considering Troy was back in 13th on the same tyre. It didn't stop me feeling that I had let everyone down. This was the biggest single day attendance for any sporting event in Britain that year. Every time I moved a muscle, the crowds in the grandstand facing the garage were on their feet. I needed to tell them how much I appreciated their support, and why I hadn't been able to bring them the win that they craved. So I went out onto the track to say how much I loved them all and still got the biggest cheer of the day.

Then I needed some space. I hadn't been able to move all weekend and the last thing I wanted to do was sign a load of autographs. I went back to the motorhome and my room in hospitality and waited for the crowds to clear, which felt like ages. I had been expected at the hotel's annual charity night, but I was in no mood for a fancy dress party. I wasn't to know, but a surprise presentation had been arranged. The organisers had presumed I would be there and, if I had won both races, I probably would have been. In the event my mum had to go up and collect it – something which annoyed a few people – as I just wanted to be a million miles away from Brands Hatch.

I was snapping at everyone and felt very claustrophobic. The heat and humidity made things even worse. I couldn't stand having to talk to people when I was in such a bad mood. All I wanted was to shut my eyes, open them again and find myself on a deserted beach. The next best thing would be for Geoff to fly me to his hotel half a mile away, where I could dive into the pool. Eventually, when my dad took the kids, we decided to go for a Chinese with Graham and Louise, and Geoff and Mandy. We piled into a car and I crouched down in the front seat, so that nobody would spot me as we fought our way through the traffic. After the meal I sneaked back into the Thistle Hotel through a back door and went straight to my room.

Geoff flew us back home the following morning and, while we sunbathed around the pool in the afternoon, we decided to join both couples for a week in Ibiza – the first summer holiday that me and Michaela had ever had.

As it was a late booking, we were on a chartered flight but the airline looked after us and made sure that we weren't bothered because I tend to have a lot of hassle in those situations. We had found an apartment on the nice side of the island, not where all the idiots stay.

In a way, it didn't help having a four-week break before the next round because this was the only time in the year when doubts started to creep into my mind. Brands was still gnawing away at me, even though I still led the championship by around 50 points. But the break did help take my mind off things. One afternoon we were at a harbour filled with fantastic £2 million yachts. I said to Graham,

'I'm going to wander around to see if anyone recognises me.' The biggest and best boat had a Union Jack on the back and, sure enough, the owner came up and said, 'It's Carl Fogarty, isn't it? Do you want to come aboard?' I was on the deck waving at everyone before he finished the word 'aboard'.

It belonged to a really nice bloke called Klaas Zwart, a multi-millionaire who owns Ascari Cars in Scotland. He also produced components for oil rigs and raced ex-Formula One cars in the Boss series. He was also a big fan and invited the rest of us aboard, after we had taken our shoes off, and allowed us to use his jet-ski and his smaller boat. In the end, I felt like we had out-stayed our welcome a bit but we arranged to go for a drink with his family that night.

The holiday was supposed to be a break to recharge my batteries, but we ended up being up until 4am every morning. And it didn't get me away from bike problems.

We went to hire some bikes on the first day and, on the way to the rental shop, walked past a bar. The owner came running out.

'I can't believe it's you. We have about 100 people in here every Sunday watching you race. Don't bother hiring a bike, you can have mine for the week,' he insisted.

'Fine,' I thought, 'that saves me paying.'

Throughout 1999 I seemed to get away without paying for anything!

He leant me his Yamaha V-Max, their version of a Harley-Davidson, which I thought I could potter around on without a problem. Geoff and Mandy hired a 600cc Yamaha Enduro bike and we set off around the island, finding nice beaches. I didn't like my bike one bit, as I'm not used to riding road bikes, whereas Geoff owns a Ducati. I could see he was itching for a go on the V-Max and I was more than happy to oblige. And he looked confident on it – for a few days.

On one of the last days, on our way back to hand in the bikes, we were on some winding roads about 8km away from the resort. Coming into one corner at only about 20–30mph, Geoff realised that he was running too wide because the bike was very difficult to lean over. As the bend tightened, he tried to lean further over but fell off right in front of me and I just missed Mandy's head (she was on the back) by anchoring the front and back brakes on. They both slid along the road. 'Oooooooh! Bare legs and arms on Tarmac. That is really going to hurt,' I cringed.

Luckily nothing was coming in the opposite direction and they stopped sliding just before the barrier, which separated the road from a sheer drop down to the sea. I parked up and ran back. Geoff had only scraped his elbow but Mandy's leg was like a slice of bacon, a big disc of raw steak. Her elbow was also a mess. She was jumping up and down shouting, 'You bloody pillock, you bloody pillock!' I thought he got off lightly. If it had been Michaela, I would have been over the cliffs.

The bike was an even bigger mess. Because it was so heavy, the bars were bent, the front brake lever had snapped off, the indicator and mirror were knackered and the exhaust was bent. Geoff and Mandy didn't want to get on it again, so it was down to me to ride it back with a very worried Michaela on the back. She nipped me every time I locked the back brake, while I struggled to steer the bent bars. To add insult to injury, we had to ride past a café packed with bikers who were at a Harley convention! They all started cheering, thinking I had been invited. As we limped back into the street the guy was stood outside his bar. At first he was smiling but, as we got nearer, his face started to drop as he noticed the damage. All I could do was state the obvious: 'There's been an accident.' He took it very well, as Geoff was not far behind and offered to pay for all the repairs.

The next job was to try and clean Mandy's wound, to prevent infection. She was climbing the walls as Michaela tried to scrub the dirt out. I knew that she wouldn't scream if I had a go. So I grabbed the brush and rubbed hard as she writhed in agony. A piece of Tarmac had even become lodged in her ankle, so we had to dig that out as well. The doctor gave her an injection to be on the safe side. It was only to be a matter of weeks before Mandy needed much more than an injection to repair the injuries from another bike accident.

All things considered, I was ready to race again by the time of the Austrian round. Edwards had tried to wind me up by saying, 'Carl always cracks under this kind of pressure.' I couldn't remember the last time I had cracked under pressure. He seemed to be forgetting that I had won three world titles in the previous five years. But what did stop me from sleeping was the rain on Saturday night. The heavens opened and it continued to rain on race day. Maybe things were starting to turn against me.

Parts of the track had started to dry by the start of the race, so we decided on cut slicks in the front and back. Edwards gambled on a cut slick in the front and a slick in the back. That would obviously suit him if the track continued to dry, which it did. Late on in the race my tyres were like destroyed slicks, but Edwards hadn't pulled away. Then it started to rain again, catching a lot of riders out, including Slight and Corser. All I had to do was keep the bike upright to clinch second, as Edwards slid all over the track in front of me to win a good race. It rained throughout the second race and we both started cautiously. But, after a few laps down in 11th, I thought, 'Bugger this! Even if I finish, I'm only going to collect four or five points.' So I started to lap about three seconds quicker and moved up past Edwards to sixth before two more riders fell off and I ended up in fourth. I had kept my cool and come through a big test.

Assen, the very next week, was my territory. If it stayed dry in Holland no one would come anywhere near me. And it was boiling hot – in front of an army of around 60,000 British fans. I was determined to concentrate on my own thing and even opted to use a tyre that nobody ever used, a different shaped 16.5inch. That also threw Troy's preparation because he had tried it but didn't like it. I was first away and led from start to finish.

Obviously, Troy switched tyre for the second race and pulled a 1.5 second lead until I was able to find a clear track in second place. The gap stayed the same for two laps until I reined in half a second per lap. He must have been thinking, 'What the hell can I do about this?' There was nothing he could do. I breezed past him and he was demoralised. It was just about the first time that I had heard another rider admit that he'd been totally helpless. 'On this circuit, there is nothing anyone can do to beat this guy,' Corser said. The crowd went bananas as I had one hand on the world championship trophy.

The sensible thing to do would have been to wrap myself in cotton wool before the following weekend's race at Hockenheim. Instead I went motocrossing on the Wednesday with a couple of mates called Garth Woods, who owns an engineering company in Blackburn, and Austin Clews. Needless to say I had a horrendous crash. The bike landed sideways after a jump, threw me off and my wrist twisted under the bike. At first I thought it was broken, then I realised that I was dazed and my neck was stiff. I was sat in the sand at Preston Docks, four days before I could clinch the world title and suddenly thought, 'What on earth are you doing? Just put the bike back in the van, go home while you are in one piece and don't tell anyone.'

My wrist was still sore when I arrived at Hockenheim, with a lead of 71 points and needing just one more win to secure the title. I was starting to feel the pressure a bit. It seemed that everyone except me had it down as a foregone conclusion. I hadn't slept well for a few weeks, I was off my food and I didn't have a lot of time for people. That's part and parcel of my dedication. When you have such a big lead, there is always a nagging doubt that you could throw it all away. I just wanted to get down to business and, if things went well, start enjoying it all on Sunday night. But things never seemed to be that simple.

I was in the paddock on Thursday afternoon with Geoff, sorting out a few last minute details before practice started the following day. Michaela and Mandy had taken a couple of scooters around the track. Mandy looked nervous, because she hadn't had much experience of riding a scooter. The next thing I knew, Michaela was running towards me screaming. 'Mandy is really hurt. There's been a terrible accident,' she shouted. 'Mandy's had a crash, I thought she was dead,' she kept repeating, almost hysterically.

Me and Geoff jumped on scooters and set off to where Michaela was pointing. One of the doctors happened to be walking across the paddock at the same time, so he jumped on the back of my bike. By the time we reached the scene there was an ambulance already there, as it had been parked opposite the spot where the accident had happened. As Michaela and Mandy were riding down the straight, the driver of one of the machines that paints the markings on the track must have just turned towards them.

Michaela, who is used to riding a scooter, managed to swerve out of the way. But Mandy panicked. The truck had a bar, to attach a lamp to, sticking out of the side and it smashed into her leg, practically slicing it off just above the ankle. Both bones had been sheared through and her foot was hanging on by a bit of muscle. She had also been thrown down the track and had landed on her head. There was blood everywhere and her teeth were smashed. She was just conscious, although Michaela said she had been knocked out at first.

I thought the worst when I saw the blood around her head. But then she groaned, 'Oh Carl, I'm never riding a bike again.' I realised then that she would be okay. I knew that the leg would heal. It's when you bang your head that you can have real problems. Within an hour everything had settled down and I had almost forgotten about the whole incident. It was the start of a big weekend for me and, to be perfectly honest, it didn't affect me in the slightest.

Mandy was taken to the nearest hospital, had a long operation to pin her leg back together and stayed in Germany for the next week. Obviously we checked on her condition every day but it wasn't something that preyed on my mind in the build-up to the races. By the time we were back in England, it was something I could even joke about. I told everyone that Michaela had tried to kill Mandy, although I'm not sure that Michaela appreciated the joke. Mandy is still having a few problems and needed a bone graft from her hip to help the fracture heal properly. The gaps between the two ends of the bone had been too wide for it to knit together and calcify properly. Then the bone developed an infection and the doctors decided to take the plates out, again hoping that would not stop the healing process. In many ways she was lucky, although she probably wished she had never met us after this and the fall in Ibiza.

Qualifying was none too smooth, either. A clutch problem during Superpole meant that I was seventh on the grid, at a track where I wouldn't be able to go easy on the bike and just pick up the points. The long straights at Hockenheim mean that there is maximum strain on the engine for long periods, and that's just to stay in the draught of other bikes. During the Sunday morning warm-up I was obviously a bit tense.

One particular fat little German marshal had annoyed me the previous day by not letting me out of pit-lane, which meant I had to stop the bike and get the mechanics to run down and start me up again. On the Sunday, I had been out on one bike and was about to go out on the number two bike. Just as I was approaching the end of pit-lane, the red light, which signals the end of the session, came on. All I wanted to do was go out, do one lap, and come back in. But the steward leapt out with his red flag and he was determined not to let me out at any cost. I almost ran into him. I was swearing like a madman although he couldn't understand a word I was saying. I backed the bike up a few yards and pretended to run straight at him, stopping just short, of course! By this stage he was crapping himself because I was still furious and giving him the finger. A woman was stood close by and she was indicating that she had seen everything that had happened. She was obviously going to love grassing me up.

When the first race eventually arrived I was confident with our choice of tyre. Again I went for the hardest that Michelin had, similar to the tyre we used throughout 1995. From what I had seen, the others were struggling and I thought I was the only one who had done a race distance in practice – and I had done it twice. Davide, watching from the pit lane, didn't think that I got off to a good start. In fact I had charged through from the second row and was leading going into the first chicane. That made me uneasy. All the time I was wondering where Troy was, because I only needed to beat him to win the title. Yet again I had to talk to myself to keep focused. 'Look, just do what you do. Keep your head down and keep putting in fast consistent laps,' I told myself.

At the start of the last lap I thought my board was telling me that Troy was in ninth. That was perfect, there was no point getting into a dice with Slight in second place. He came past and was weaving all over expecting me to come back at him. I wasn't interested in him in the slightest and was looking behind just to make sure Troy wasn't there – but knowing that the world title was mine. For once in my life I wasn't bothered about winning the race and crossed the line in second with a big wheelie. I stopped the bike in front of the grandstand, where there were around 30,000 Brits who had made the journey. I punched the air and then dropped to my knees in the sand saying little prayers of thanks.

The T-shirts were out in pit-lane saying, 'Carl Fogarty: Four times world champion' and I noticed, behind the podium, that Aaron Slight was furious. Someone came up to me and said, 'You've won the race!'

'No, Aaron won the race,' I said, confused.

It turned out that the red flags had been out on the final lap after an accident, which meant that the result stood from the start of the last lap when I was leading. It was a bit embarrassing but I didn't care because I had won the title.

Slight didn't appear on the podium and I probably would have done the same because he won the race fair and square. He made a protest but it was rejected. And, as far as I was concerned, the trouble with the marshal from the morning had also been forgotten. But team manager Davide Tardozzi had been ordered up to race control. The organisers originally wanted to fine me 3,000 Swiss Francs, until I was talked into going up there to apologise to everyone and they settled for 1,000 Swiss Francs, about £400. It was no skin off my nose.

The relief during the break between races was amazing. Davide had to remind me that there was another race because I turned up at the garage with a big grin.

But, as soon as my helmet was on, there was no smiling. It was back to business as usual, although Chili just edged me into second in a good race. The Alstare Suzuki team threw a big party in the paddock, with some strippers, but I had an early flight in the morning and there would be plenty more celebrations back home. So we didn't have a really late night in Germany. A few press were waiting at the airport again, including a right nugget from the *Manchester Evening News*. He knew that I had won a world title, but did not know whether I rode a bike or a snail. I could have won the tiddlywinks world title for all he cared.

I had been in a mischievous mood after the Hockenheim races and told the press that I wouldn't be travelling to Japan for the final race a month later. There was never any doubt that I would be going, but Ducati took me seriously and had a quiet word. As it turned out, there was some doubt the week before the final race because a nuclear leak threatened the event in Sugo. We were due to travel on the bullet train from Tokyo through the affected area, but Ducati made a lot of checks and we were promised that everything would be okay. It was a pity, as I really could have done without that extra round.

Michaela felt exactly the same . . .

## CHAPTER EIGHTEEN

# *Teamwork*

Michaela picked her moment to suggest that there was no point in her travelling to Japan, but I was busy with something else, so I ignored her. She tried again.

'Carl, you don't really need me in Japan, do you?'

Again I didn't respond.

'I guess I'm coming to Japan, then!'

'Yep, you're coming to Japan,' I grinned.

She was right, there was no real need for her to travel halfway across the world for a meaningless race. But I've come to rely on her company at races and she has been at every round for the last couple of years. That's a measure of the strength of our relationship. Unlike many couples, who go off to work at the start of each day and maybe spend a couple of hours together in the evening and at weekends, Michaela and I are in each other's pockets for the most part of most days. It's got to the stage that I don't feel right at a meeting if she is not there.

It can be a very lonely time in a foreign country, and especially somewhere like Japan, during a race meeting. The mechanics stay behind at the track working on the bike, so the rider has to go back to a hotel room or go out and eat alone. It's so important to have somebody there to share a joke with or provide a shoulder to cry on. Michaela and I know each other inside out and the relationship has matured over the years. Anyone who knows us will say that we are two very strong characters. We both let people know exactly what we think about them. That can be a potentially explosive combination and obviously there are flash points. It has occasionally come to blows but I always warn her that I'll never let the fight end until I've won!

There was a period when a big row meant we could go for days without speaking. But, the more Michaela has become involved with the business side of things, the harder it is to ignore each other and now we don't argue as much as we used to. Nowadays I can recognise when I've been unreasonable. Perhaps I might have snapped at her if she was in my chair in the garage after I had been out during qualifying when things hadn't gone to plan. But her mood will soon tell me when I've overstepped the mark and I usually end up eating humble pie.

It might be a sign that I am mellowing because, more often than not, I'm now the first to apologise – in my own way. I might mutter, 'Dickhead!' as we pass in the corridor, to try and break the ice. I actually try to avoid arguments at all costs but she sometimes pushes me to the brink and forces me to say something nasty. Days later, when it's all forgotten as far as I'm concerned, she will throw it back in my face and force an apology out of me.

Michaela loved to be involved with the team. Ever since around 1993 she was a regular on the pit wall, noting down my lap times for the records. A lot of the wives and girl-friends take a back seat, but Michaela was always in and around the garage and therefore on television. So she now has a high profile of her own now and is often recognised in England when I'm not there. The Italians loved our public shows of emotion after races and that's perhaps one of the reasons I'm so popular in that country.

Her presence also served another purpose. Biking has

always attracted a glamorous female following. Around the time I first started seeing Michaela, I found it quite hard to pull girls even though I was racing all over the world. I'm no model – I suppose I'm just an average-looking guy with distinctive features. It's a similar thing with Mick Jagger – people either think that you're good-looking or that you're an ugly git. Either way, it doesn't bother me. I've always had good-looking girlfriends and I've got a beautiful wife, so there must be something there that women like. Now it would be relatively easy to pull birds because I'm well known and have a bit of cash. But, because Michaela and the kids are always around, everyone sees that I'm a big family man. So perhaps girls don't want to get involved and leave me well alone. Sure, they occasionally give me the eye, but there have certainly never been crowds of them rushing into the garage trying to rip my pants off.

That's not to say that Michaela doesn't get a bit insecure. Perhaps I do sometimes have wandering eyes. Show me a man who hasn't. So Michaela will ask, 'What's she got that I haven't?' I'll say 'Nothing. I'm married to you, though.'

It's just not in my nature to tell her she looks beautiful all the time, so she hates it when I say that some stranger looks sexy. When a girl once asked me in the Isle of Man to sign her boob right across the nipple, she went apeshit. And she hates it whenever I'm asked to do something like squirt water on the contestants in a Miss Wet T-shirt contest (although it's okay if she's allowed to judge the Mr Willy competition). But that's about the only temptation that is put in my way, which is fine by me. There is just too much to throw away, even if I was tempted. Many sportsmen can't resist affairs and you read about it in the papers every Sunday morning. It's not as bad in motorcycle racing as many people think, and nowhere near as bad as it is in football.

A lot of the other superbike riders are in the same boat, as most have wives or steady girlfriends. The younger riders, who haven't got someone in tow, are generally not famous enough to attract the interest in the first place. One or two who do have partners still play the field and get away with it, but that's their business. Sometimes I wish it had been laid on a plate when I was younger and still in the market. But if that had been the case I would probably be washed up and living in some flat in Monaco with a drug problem – with a different woman every night. You can't have your cake and eat it and I think I'll settle for what I've got, thanks very much.

Michaela's involvement with the team was a way of controlling her nerves, more than anything. It's always worse for people who are watching because they can't do anything about what's happening on the track. At least I was in a position to influence things. It wasn't that she was scared, just anxious that I didn't injure myself and, at the same time, keen for me to do well. She knew only too well that I was not a nice person for a couple of days after a bad result. But, while I knew she's a nervous wreck, it was calming for me to have her around and especially when things got tense.

I realise that I wasn't always the easiest bloke to be around, as I wanted everything done to perfection. And if I were to ask for a cup of tea at home I'd probably be told to go and get it myself. At first she was like that at races, and a proper pain in the arse. But she grew to appreciate the pressures that I was under, with everyone wanting a slice of my time, and knew that it was not worth arguing. So she started to do more and more stuff, such as mixing up drinks or fetching tablets from the doctors – the type of things that I always used to do for myself. But there were certain things, like seeing to my helmet visor, which I still preferred to do myself so that nobody else could be blamed if it wasn't done properly.

Michaela has also got a lot better at the business side of things, which she hated at first but is now very comfortable with. She can be a very tough negotiator and runs my diary. I've never seen the sense in employing an agent and having to give him a 10 per cent cut of every deal, although Neil Bramwell, who helped with this book, is now arranging more and more promotional work with us. That was all becoming too much for us to handle, so it's nice for someone to take that pressure off. Michaela was also my first line of defence from the telephone. So she was heavily involved when all the shit kicked off with my uncle Brian, my dad's brother.

The problem dated back to around 1994 when Brian asked me if he could try and make a bit of cash selling pieces of pottery, plates and mugs with my name and pictures on. I was only too pleased to help out because he seemed to have struggled for most of his life. Even when he did enjoy a rare bit of luck, Brian always seemed to do something stupid and blow it. For four or five years, he would set up a stall at race meetings and sell a few items – so everyone went away happy. I never asked for a cut and didn't want a share of the proceeds. He then fell in with some people who set themselves up as Foggy Promotions, an offshoot of Motorsport Enterprises, claiming to be the official suppliers of Carl Fogarty merchandise.

A professional outfit called Clinton Enterprises, run by Tim Clinton, who also represented Castrol Honda, had handled all my official merchandising for a number of years. But suddenly they were being told that Foggy Promotions had the sole rights to my merchandise. That was bullshit but Brian and these guys were by then driving round in a car with all kinds of slogans painted on the side, not to mention producing caps and T-shirts which they had no right to do. They even used the logo of my eyes, which Alan Pendry has exclusive rights to use after copyrighting the logo, which was based on the design owned by No Fear and looks like a Polo mint broken in half and pulled apart.

Then they set up a new web site on the internet with the message, supposedly from me, saying, 'This is my official range of products that I endorse. Welcome to my web site. I would also like to thank my Uncle Brian for supporting me throughout my career.' This was totally untrue.

This had all blown up in the middle of the 1999 championship and I didn't want it to distract me from my racing. So I told Brian, 'You can't do this. I'll have a meeting with you and your people once the season is over.' In all honesty though, I had no intention of getting involved. I just wanted to shut them up for the time being. So, during the week after my victory at Hockenheim, it all kicked off when I was out in Italy helping to promote the Milan Bike Show. I had enough mayhem to deal with out there, without all this. Shark had asked me to sign some helmets on a specially constructed stage but had advertised the time that I would be there. It was a big mistake because Italians never form an orderly queue. I had only signed one before the crowd burst through the security and the stage collapsed. I was practically picked up by my bodyguards and carried to safety!

That night, Michaela rang me to say that Brian had warned Clinton that he wouldn't be able to sell merchandise at an event that was being organised by Blackburn Council to commemorate my fourth world title. A similar tribute night had been held every championship year, but the previous year's had turned into a big autograph session. I was uncomfortable with this because people had paid for tickets and thought I was profiting, which was not the case. But this year the night had become the focus of this running battle for my merchandising rights.

I went ballistic, so Michaela rang Brian to tell him exactly how I felt. He flew off the handle with Michaela. 'I can do whatever I want,' he said. 'I have a contract with Carl that gives me his worldwide rights. Anyway, it's got nothing to do with you. I have got permission off the Fogarty family,' he ranted. Again it was all bullshit.

The day after I returned home I received a recorded delivery letter from Motorsport Enterpises, which was also sent to Ducati, Action Performance and Clinton. It claimed they held all my worldwide rights because I had signed a piece of paper in 1995 allowing Brian to sell 'pottery'. Apparently, I had signed it because Brian was getting hassle from some of the circuits who were asking for official documents before allowing him to sell his stuff. But Motorsport Enterprises went on to claim that 'pottery' was just a trading name, which included all forms of merchandise. And *they* threatened to take *me* to court if I didn't co-operate.

I flipped. Just at that moment, dad rang. The timing was all wrong.

'What are you doing about this celebration evening at Blackburn? Alf Wright from the council is trying to get it all sorted,' he asked in all innocence.

'I am not going to that fucking thing because of your bastard brother. I'm going to kill him,' I shouted. 'And if you've got anything to do with it, you can fuck off as well.'

Dad was obviously upset with the way I had spoken to him. But I thought that he'd taken Brian's side. I didn't speak to dad again until Christmas Day, when he turned up with presents for the kids. You could have cut the atmosphere with a knife. 'There's a present for you. That should cheer you up,' he said and off he went. The Blackburn event was eventually cancelled using the legitimate excuse that the council hadn't even checked whether I was available for that particular night.

Actually, I had already decided to switch to Action Performance for the year 2000 before all this blew up, as they handled a lot of World Superbike and Ducati merchandise. There is the potential to make a lot of money on the back of my name but, in the wrong hands, there is also potential for a lot of people, including the public, to be ripped off. So my lawyers, and those of Action Performance and Ducati, were on the case in an increasingly complicated battle. 'Brian said you would let us do this and Brian said we could do that,' a guy called Warren Cox, from Motorsport Enterprises, moaned before backing off and offering to try and come to an amicable arrangement, claiming that no one would benefit in the long run. 'I don't give a fuck what Brian said, you're getting nothing out of me,' I said. I couldn't understand how anyone, least of all my own uncle, would have the nerve to sell my stuff without my consent.

Out of the blue, towards the end of January, dad phoned up and asked if he could come round so that I could sign some posters. He turned up, I signed the posters and, again, he left with hardly a word said between us. I couldn't believe what was happening. Dad rang again a couple of weeks later but this time to say that he had been in contact with Barry Marsden, a Blackburn businessman who had a history of being involved with failed companies. Marsden said he was something to do with a company called Harvest.

This company had offered to buy the agreement off Motorsport Enterprises. Harvest claimed to have offices in Blackburn, Texas and Singapore and dad told me they had great ideas to make all sorts of products like a Foggy Plug, Foggy Flex and a Foggy Watch.

'I want nothing to do with them,' I said. 'You haven't been around for the last four months, so how would you know how far this has gone and how much trouble Brian has caused.'

'Well you said all those bad things to me,' he replied.

At last we had started a conversation and it was clear that dad had no idea of the scale of the problem. He went mad and went straight round to Brian's and told him to stop it all. Brian refused and whined that he hadn't been able to sleep for four months. It was obvious that Brian had misled everyone and dug himself into a big hole. I'll never speak to him again and he has also pissed off the people he got involved with, as they had spent money on the back of his promises.

Meanwhile, some of my people had been doing some digging on Harvest. Apparently, it wasn't until they had read a story in the *Lancashire Evening Telegraph* that they realised my uncle was acting without my consent. So I spoke to their main man, a Cheshire-based businessman called John H Gee, to try and make some progress. He seemed nice enough but, by then, I didn't know who to trust. I told him that, if he had commercial ideas, I was prepared to listen to them as long as they had nothing to do with Motorsport Enterprises or Brian Fogarty. But, after another story in the *Telegraph*, Harvest quickly disappeared out of the equation.

By then I didn't care if I never sold another piece of merchandising. I was determined not to let these people make any money from my name. At one stage, just a month before the season, I was considering not racing in the year 2000. The previous four months had been a living night-mare. It had caused tension between me and Michaela because, as is often the case, you take things like this out on those closest to you. And that wasn't fair on her. I told Ducati, 'I really don't want to race this year. What's the point in me racing when all this is going on. I'm not riding round a track and risking my life when these bastards could make money out of me.' That pricked up Ducati's ears and they sprang into action. A crisis meeting was called between their lawyers, those of Action Performance and my own legal team, when it was agreed to take Motorsport Enterprises to court.

In the end, it didn't come to that as we agreed to settle out of court by paying Brian and his mates £20,000 to get out of my life. Ducati agreed to foot half the bill and it was probably the best £10,000 I have ever spent because I never have to deal with the man again. The money would probably not have even covered their legal fees, so at least they were not making any profit out of me. And, while there's no doubt that we would have won a court battle, there did not seem any point spending so much money on lawyers. The whole thing taught me a valuable lesson, never to trust anyone in the future. Even Action Performance let me down, by cancelling three quarters of my merchandising contract with them because of the crash and the fact that I hadn't been racing.

At least everything was cleared up with dad. He had played a big part in my career and was always there to support me in the early years. Before all this blew up, he'd always been easy-going, laid back and, apart from the odd row at race meetings in the heat of the moment, we had never really fallen out for any length of time before. He has obviously been very proud of me from the day I was born – you can tell that by my middle name, George. Personally, I think middle names are snobby and cannot see the point of them because you're never going to lose your first name so our two do not have them.

Generally, he doesn't have a bad word for anyone and nobody seems to have a bad word for him. That wasn't always the case. While he was building up his business, dad and Phillip had a reputation as being pretty ruthless. Dad is certainly not the type to let anyone stand in his way if he wants something badly enough. Throughout their early life, all four brothers were in trouble for one thing or another like fighting.

That business developed into a very successful haulage and storage business with huge clients like Star Paper Mill, the Thwaites brewery, and Walkersteel, run by the late Jack Walker. It became a bit of a goldmine, especially when they moved to a site nearer to the town centre and right next to a rail link.

Phillip gradually lost interest and, in 1989, they decided to sell out to a company called Gilbraith's. Dad stayed on as a consultant for another five years before packing up altogether. But he isn't the type to sit around kicking his heels and helped a lot with work on our last two houses. Even now he helps a couple of people with their gardens, always wearing his Carl Fogarty T-shirt!

In fact, everything he walks round in is the old stuff that I've thrown out. He begrudges buying anything for himself, and thinks it's disgusting if I buy a pair of pants for £60 or £70. Dad is much happier going to some cheap shop and picking up a pair for £10.99. He's not tight, because he loves to buy the kids stuff. It's back to the work ethic thing. He hates thinking he is making someone else well off, without them doing anything for it. So he will always try and repair something rather than call in an expert, which usually results in it costing him more money in the long run when it breaks down again. If, for instance, he wanted a new tennis racket, he'd pay £14.99 thinking he has got value for money even if it only lasted a few games. So I've tended to buy him things like that for Christmas.

I was also sick of seeing him driving around in a heap of a car, a Land Rover, that he had bought from the auctions. It was always breaking down and, whenever dad went into a garage, he tried to flog it in part exchange for another 'bargain'. So, one Christmas, I bought him a Land Cruiser Colorado jeep from a dealer in Northampton (because I wanted one as well!)

It was a £30,000 turbodiesel automatic and a gorgeous deep blue colour – and I threw in an 8 FOG number plate. On Christmas Eve I made an excuse that I wanted to borrow his heap to pick up some presents for the kids, but took it away and flogged it for around £7,000. That evening I told him that it was too late to return his car and that he could pick it up when they came for Christmas dinner. When they arrived on Christmas Day I said, 'Can you go and get your bloody car out of my garage. I can't get that pile of shit to start.'

'Why? There's nothing wrong with it. You've just got to turn the key the right way,' he muttered as he trudged off to the garage.

When he opened the door he saw this brand new jeep, all carefully wrapped up with ribbons and a big message 'Merry Xmas Dad'. He thought I had bought it for myself, and couldn't figure it out that it was for him. 'It's yours, you daft git,' I told him. It is the only time I have seen tears in his eyes. And I've got the moment on video to prove it. It made me so happy because he had done so much for us down the years. My relationship with mum, who was an orphan and has two brothers living in South Africa and the States, has never really been that close.

Mum and dad split up around July 1998. Until a year or so before that they used to follow me all over the world, supporting me. Or, if it wasn't possible to travel, they would stay at home and look after the kids. Mum would be very nervous watching me and I'll always remember one video-tape shot of her, after I had fallen at the other side of the

Daytona track in 1990 and word had not reached the pits whether I was okay. She went off on her own to gaze through fencing, obviously worried sick.

It was not a bitter divorce and didn't affect me at all. They were just two people who had grown apart and out of love. The only thing they really had in common as a couple was mine and dad's racing and that had obviously finished. When their kids left home they realised there was no real reason to stay together any longer. But they are still on friendly terms and, at Brands a couple of years ago, dad turned up with his new girlfriend, Bev, and mum didn't bat an eyelid.

Mum has actually just moved into Georgina's old house. Me and Georgina were always fighting as kids and nothing much seems to have changed. She was an annoying little sister and I probably picked on her a bit. I'm not sure that many boys get on well with their younger sisters as a general rule. But it was probably quite cool for her to have an older brother, although she would probably not admit that. There were the obvious benefits for me in meeting her friends but that worked both ways because she went out with a couple of racers, Nigel Bosworth and Darren Dixon, while I was riding 250ccs. Now she seems to copy everything we do. She married Simon Bradshaw, who runs a car valeting and dry cleaning business in Blackburn, seven months after we were married. She had children soon after we had children and seems incapable of doing anything on her own.

Mum and my sister can both be a bit childish and have caused a few problems down the years. Perhaps they have always been a bit spoilt because dad did too much for them. They are constantly falling out with each other, their own friends, and Michaela. That's because they don't seem to realise that Michaela leads a busy life and likes to see her own friends. But, out of the blue, they will ring up and say,

'You haven't rung for ages. I find that really annoying.'

This has gone on for about 10 years and there's no need for it. Maybe my sister in particular is a little bit jealous of our lifestyle. I've tried to help financially where I could, lending Georgina and her husband some money to set up their business and helping mum to buy that house. I would now rather help my mate Howard, who works his balls off day in, day out, to buy a tractor for his farm rather than help some members of my own family. There are more important things in life than tittle-tattle gossip, or moaning about your hair, weight or clothes, not to mention other people's hair, weight and clothes. I'm sure that they don't realise that their comments upset people a lot of the time.

My dad and Michaela's dad, Alan, are two very different people. But we would be knackered without Alan and Pat. Whenever we're away they move into the house and keep the ship afloat. We don't even have to ask them to help out, fixing and organising things and even cleaning up. Without their help and support Michaela wouldn't have been able to travel to the races because we would have to pay someone to look after the kids. They are also always babysitting and the girls love it when they stay. So that's another reason why it has made sense to stay in Blackburn, as the girls mean everything to us.

Danielle and Claudia are like chalk and cheese. Danielle is the prim and proper lady and has to win at everything she does. She was competing in a running race at a village fete a few years ago and was winning until another girl passed her shortly before the finishing line. Danielle stopped dead in her tracks and started crying. I asked her, 'What did you do that for?'

'I wasn't going to win. That other girl was,' she said.

'You can't just do that, you have to take part,' I lectured. Michaela sniggered in the background, 'I wonder who she takes after?' She was right. I would never take part in individual school sports that I didn't think I was any good at. And, like Danielle, I used to be quite shy and guarded with strangers.

She also seems to have been born with my inability to concentrate for long periods of time at school. She is not bad at any subject, although they are both having private maths lessons during the week, but tends to be middle of the class rather than excelling. The other kids at her school, a private school for girls in Blackburn, are at the age when they see me on telly and realise that their friend's daddy is famous. That tends to make our two both pretty popular in the playground. Neither of them would bat an eyelid if I appeared on the screen out of the blue. In fact they would probably look the other way!

My fame has helped bring Danielle out of her shell to a certain extent. She can see that being in front of the cameras is not unusual and at the end she was happier joining me on the rostrum, whereas a couple of years ago she wouldn't have dreamed of it. When I did the double in Misano, the two of them became separated after the first race and Claudia was plonked in front of the cameras wearing a silly red crown while Danielle was trapped behind the barrier. It would have taken an army of stewards to prevent her from squirming between the legs, under the cordon and into the limelight.

In contrast to Danielle, Claudia is a bit of a tomboy and they react so differently, even to very ordinary situations. For instance, one day Geoff flew us all up to Lockerbie for Sunday lunch and the waitress asked the kids what they wanted to drink. Because it was a nice place, Danielle ordered a cup of tea while Claudia went straight for the Coke. She tends to be much more open and comfortable with other people, especially strangers.

There is a portrait photograph of the four of us hanging

over the mantelpiece in the living room, taken by a photographer from the Lake District called Annabel Williams. It captures the difference between them perfectly. Claudia has her arms draped around Michaela's neck, while Danielle sits like a grown up next to me. Claudia is much more loving, like her mum, and will always remind you of how much she loves you. But she is also very clumsy (like her mum). If there is anything to break or knock over, Claudia will find it and there are very few days that go by without something coming to grief. But she will have a go at anything because she has no fear of losing. The worrying thing is that she already drinks like a fish (again like her mum). Even at four years of age, she can down a glass of wine or beer in the blink of an eye and not show any effects (unlike her mum). Danielle would never go near the stuff.

A lot people had the impression that, because I was away racing all the time, I might not have been able to spend enough time with the girls. In fact, the opposite was true. During the season I was often abroad from Thursday to Monday. But, for the rest of the time, I was at home a lot and could take them to school and pick them up. Many dads leave for work before their kids are out of bed and get home after they're in bed. I actually probably spent more time with them when they came to watch me race, because they realised I was the centre of attention and they wanted a piece of the action. They wanted to ride on my scooter and help out in the garage. They loved to hand out posters in front of the hospitality area and serve people with drinks. When we were back home, their attitude was 'Dad's here again. I'd rather play with my toys.'

I suppose I can be quite strict with them, perhaps more so than Michaela, and it drives me daft when they fight. More often than not it's because Danielle is bossing Claudia, trying to stop her being a pest. If sending them to their rooms doesn't work, then they know that a slap is on the way. But the result is that we can take them anywhere in public and they will be as good as gold. There are perhaps not that many parents who could say that with confidence.

It's just a shame that the same can't always be said about some adults. We were at Donington for the race in 1998 and had arrived a day early for the Thursday press conferences. I went up to the track, while Michaela took the kids into Nottingham city centre. She had just parked up on the multi-storey when a bloke approached her and asked her the time. She immediately didn't like the look of him and thought he was going to try and snatch her Rolex watch.

But as she was looking at the time, he whipped open his coat and said, 'What can you do with this?' Michaela panicked a bit and just dragged the kids out of the way and ran off. If she had been on her own she'd have probably shouted, 'Is that all you've got?', kneed him in the balls and knocked his head off. Luckily the girls did not see anything and did not know what had gone on. But I was livid when I found out. Michaela reported it to the police and the bloke had apparently done it a few times. He was picked up that afternoon and later sent to prison.

It just goes to show that you can never have a totally safe environment for your kids to grow up in. There was even an incident this year, just down the road from our house in the middle of the countryside, when shots were fired at one car from another. Of course, because we lived nearby, it made the front page of the paper. Police initially thought it was rival drug gangs but later told us that the whole incident had been staged so that one of the gangs could gain some street credibility.

It's easy to say people like that should be locked up. But I don't tend to pay much attention to politics. I don't think I've ever voted and perhaps it's time I started taking a bit more notice. It pissed me off, though, when I found out that Blackburn council would not give me their highest honour – the freedom of the borough – when I retired. The best they could offer was a civic medal. I know a lot of sportsmen who have been awarded the freedom of their town for doing a lot less than I have. Apparently Blackburn only awarded the freedom of the borough to politicians, like Barbara Castle. And I thought she trained dogs!

# CHAPTER NINETEEN

# *Race Weekend*

Winter used to be a time when I could wind down and recharge my batteries for the season ahead. Away from the day-to-day pressures of racing, I could try and be a nice person again. But even without all the upset caused by the battle with my uncle, it felt like I didn't get a minute's peace after the 1999 season. If anything, I was even more in demand than I was during the racing season.

Luckily, my contract for the 2000 campaign had been sorted out long before the end of the previous season. The figures were agreed at Brands and it was a lot easier getting the right money out of Ducati than usual. It was basically agreed in a 10-minute phone call to Domenicali, but the deal was kept quiet until Hockenheim because Corser's future was not as clear. All the way through the season there had been press reports suggesting I would move away, including one that Suzuki had offered me £3 million. I might have made it sound as though they were interested, but there was no approach.

It was no great shock when the news was announced that I would be returning to Ducati. But there was one surprise still in store. Following the final races in Sugo, Ducati announced that Corser would not be re-signed for the following year. Instead they went for a talented young

American rider called Ben Bostrom, who had looked fast at the Laguna Seca round.

There were suggestions that the American owners of Ducati wanted to expand the profile of their company in the States. But Troy had also asked for stupid money, and you can only do that if you are the world champion. On top of all that, Ducati were not impressed by his performance in Japan. While I battled away, with nothing at stake, to finish second and fifth, Troy was way down the field in eighth and 14th. He had still been in with a chance of making it a Ducati one-two at the top of the championship, but allowed Edwards to draw level on points and become runner-up because he had more race wins.

I also realised that Ducati were about to make another change to the team. Every year I'd had a battle to keep Slick on and there had been more problems again during 1999. Some of the other mechanics had complained about his work and Davide was not happy with some of his behaviour at hotels and his appearance on race day. I could have dug my heels in and insisted that he stayed but I had already sensed that Slick was no longer happy. His heart wasn't in being somewhere that he wasn't wanted. His role had changed so much that he was almost just in the background. And I felt sorry for him. 'I don't want you just to be there for me. I want you to do something for yourself. You know that Ducati don't really want you, so I don't think you really want to be there either,' I told him. He came to stay in Blackburn for a few days and was pretty upset. But racing has changed and maybe Slick hasn't changed with it.

He has made it hard for himself at times, although he was always dedicated to Carl Fogarty more than any other person in racing. That might not have gone down well with people at Honda or Ducati because he always wanted to do what was right for me and not necessarily the team. And he didn't care who he upset along the way. But it was sad and strange to start the 2000 season without him. Ducati offered him a job in the factory, but that wasn't Slick. He also had a few other options and I would like to have seen him set up his own business on the back of my success. Instead, I think he took the easy option by going to work for another team, Level 3, run by Ray Stringer, with Michael Rutter and Paul Young riding Yamahas.

Going from one of the biggest teams in the world to a privately-run Yamaha team was never going to be easy. Slick must have been frustrated and started to shout his mouth off, so it didn't last long. For the 2001 season he was due to team up with Scott Russell in the American championship, working on Ducatis. He always got on well with Scott because they are both party animals, so it was anybody's guess how that would work out. They would either get on like a house on fire all year – or it would kick off straight away. But he has to be careful that he does not lose all credibility and start running out of options.

Almost straight after the Sugo round there was a test in Croatia. It rained for the whole two days and was a waste of time. Then it was Foggy Day at the NEC Bike Show, organised by MCN, where a lot of people were disappointed because I couldn't cope with the demands on my time. I had a 20-minute slot racing someone on a video game, then a 15-minute auction, and then autograph sessions when I knew I wouldn't get through half the queue. It became one mad rush with four big bodyguards keeping people away. And that doesn't go down well with the fans. I tried my best in an exhausting and hectic schedule but there is only so much you can do in a day.

Some of the money raised from the auction went towards Princess Anne's Riders For Health appeal, which I presented to her in London at a later date. She tried to tell me that the

Badminton Horse Trials are the biggest single-day attended sporting event in Britain. I put her right! Auctions are the best way for me to help charities because I am just too busy to do personal appearances and visits to injured riders in hospital. I get letters every day, addressed to 'Carl Fogarty, Blackburn', asking for signed photos but I have to admit that most don't get a reply. There are just too many to go through.

But I did manage to start a leg of Ian Botham's walk from John O'Groats to Land's End in Bristol. When I was chatting to Botham, and picking up a few blisters, it was clear we had a lot in common. When he was at his peak, he didn't train anywhere near as hard as the others. He was able to beat them because he was the best. The same went for me for a long time, although I did a bit more preparation as my career went on.

For instance, this year I did a week's motocross riding during a break in Tenerife between the Misano and Valencia tests, which set me up nicely. It's the only thing, along with trail riding, which I can motivate myself to do, as I don't like mountain biking and, while I've built a gymnasium at home, it bores the shit out of me. I'm trying to do more enduro riding and now have even more incentive after Michelin bought me a brand new KTM bike for winning the world championship and a Blackburn company, CCM, gave me a trail bike. Michaela now has a job promoting their company – it's about time she brought some money in! – and her latest idea is to get a road licence for riding bikes, so that she can come with me. I can't ever see her riding a bike on the road – she's not even safe driving a car! And we would only fall out because we're very competitive at sport. We play a lot of tennis and I always win, despite the fact that she has had lessons for two years. She reckons she's a better swimmer and sprinter – but it's not true!

The highlights of my TV dates were my second *A Question of Sport* appearance and *Through the Keyhole*, which must have been a nightmare for Lloyd Grossman to film as he wandered round our house.

The first thing you see as you walk through the door is my 1998 championship-winning bike in the hallway. And the rest of the house is packed with biking stuff like my leathers, trophies, a wicker bike and a lethal little two-stroke mini moto, which Danielle rides up and down the drive. Sure enough, the panel didn't take long to say, 'There has only been one racer who has done anything since Barry Sheene and that's . . .' I was sure they were going to say something like Ron Haslam!

Before a week's testing in Australia we managed to squeeze in a few breaks for ourselves. In January I went skiing for the first time in Italy. I absolutely loved it, despite a big fall on the first day in which I damaged my left shoulder ligaments because I was trying to keep up with Davide. If the scheduled first round in Valencia had not been cancelled because of the Spanish elections, I might not have been ready for the season.

But the highlight of the winter was a visit to Bahrain, as guest of their Crown Prince, to help promote the launch of a new powerboat by watching an attempt to go round the island in a record time. There was no existing record to beat, so it seemed a bit pointless. I was quite nervous when we arrived at the palace but the Prince broke the ice straight away when he said, 'Hi Carl. I've been following your career since 1992.' Somehow, I couldn't see Prince Charles knowing so much about his sporting guests. Formula One driver Mika Salo and his Japanese wife Noriko were also there and we were treated like royalty the whole week. They took us riding bikes in the desert, and provided a horse for Michaela.

One morning we went diving for pearls. We just snorkelled on the surface but Salo and Noriko had scuba licences. When they toppled backwards over the side of the boat, she went down headfirst with her feet stuck out of the water, flapping around. Everyone else was really concerned but I had to run to the other side of the boat, crying with laughter. Then they couldn't get her weights right and she kept bobbing back up to the surface.

All this made her seasick and, when she clambered back on board, she looked like a drowned rat. 'Ooooh, seeeek, seeeek,' she groaned, as she puked everywhere. She curled up in a corner, as sick as a dog and shivering. The devils in my head were telling me to go ahead and laugh aloud, but I managed to cover my head in my hands and run to the other end of the boat again.

There's no doubt that I've got an evil streak because I always tend to laugh at other people's misfortunes. If someone had broken a leg, it wouldn't be funny, but anything like that, which is not too serious, I always find amusing. Salo was a decent bloke, but a bit of a dominant character with his wife. And, if we ever said something was nice like a jet-ski, he was quick to say, 'Yes, I've got one at home – well, two actually.' I don't tend to bump into the Formula One guys too often but, when I do, I always get on well with Eddie Irvine. He is also a friend of Alan Pendry.

When it came to the end of March, I had almost forgotten that I had to go out and race. The test at Phillip Island was also pretty much a waste of time because I caught some kind of virus out there. At first I thought it was the food on the plane but I realised it wasn't food poisoning when I was constipated for three days. It wasn't until the final day that I began to feel better and I nearly killed Colin Edwards in the end of testing press conference when I let off three days' worth of farts.

At the next test in Misano things started to click for us. I was joint fastest with Edwards after the three days and continued that form in Valencia when I was fastest until I had a big crash on the afternoon of the second day. When I realised that I wouldn't be able to take one corner I ran off into the gravel, expecting it to slow me down. It didn't and I ditched the bike with the barrier fast approaching. I must have fallen awkwardly because I damaged ligaments in my right shoulder and knocked myself out for a few moments – for only the second time in my career. It meant that I missed the final day of the Valencia test, when Edwards on the new twin cylinder VTR1000 set a faster time. He was obviously going to be the one to look out for. And, for the first time, the Honda riders would not be able to moan that the two-cylinder Ducatis were better than their two-cylinder bikes.

Honda had to change Edwards' team-mate at the last minute after Aaron Slight was taken ill following the tests at Phillip Island. It was discovered that he had a small brain haemorrhage and he needed brain surgery in Sydney. At the time, I couldn't really see Aaron racing again, which was sad, even though I didn't get on with him. No one would have liked to see a good rider finish his career like that. Simon Crafar was hired by Honda to take Slight's place for the first few races. My shoulder injury meant that I had to cancel another brief skiing trip, to Bormio in Italy, to present the trophy on behalf of our sponsor Infostrada to the winner of the World Cup downhill. That trip was planned for just two weeks before the opening round in Kyalami, so it was perhaps for the best. Even so, when it came to leaving for Kyalami, the shoulder was still very sore and worrying me.

I don't think many people realise the drag that these long journeys can be. Bike racing is certainly not always the glamorous lifestyle that it's cracked up to be. For instance, this trip started on the Tuesday afternoon before the race and it upset Michaela when Danielle burst into tears when she dropped her off at school in the morning. We took a connecting flight from Manchester to Heathrow, where British Airways at least try to make life a bit easier. They had spotted that I was on the flight and a guy met us at the other end to bypass the transfer between terminals by driving us there directly. Then we were upgraded from Business Class to First Class, which often happens, so at least we had a bed and some free pyjamas! But I didn't sleep too well on the 11-hour flight to Johannesburg because I couldn't get comfortable with my shoulder. To add insult to injury the captain wished the Honda team, who were on the same flight, the best of luck for Sunday's race!

We were met at the airport and, in pouring rain, driven to our hotel in a Bentley by a guy who owns a Ferrari dealership near Johannesburg. Then I went straight up to the track in the afternoon to see the doctors about my shoulder. The injury had meant that I hadn't been able to do any motocross riding in the build-up to the first race so I made a token effort and went for a run around the track with a friend.

Davide was also worried about the shoulder and arranged a scan in Pretoria. After hanging round at the hospital for hours, the machine broke while I was inside! So all the next day was spent back at the track with the doctors and physios, trying to find out exactly what was wrong. The initial diagnosis was that I had torn some cartilage in the rotator cuff of the joint and I had a painkilling injection in my backside – which I hate – but it seemed to help.

South Africa, and Johannesburg in particular, is not a place where you can wander round and experiment with where to eat and drink. All the hotels and houses are protected by barbed wire and the crime is so high that you stick with what you know. So we went back to Montego Bay in the main square of the huge Sandton City shopping centre, where you feel safe enough – apart from one waitress who was after tickets for Sunday. When we went back on the Thursday, the owner gave us the meal on the house. My new team-mate, Ben, and his girlfriend at the time, Leeann Tweeden, a model and TV presenter from Los Angeles, also ate there on the first night. We had all been winding Michaela up that she now had some competition on the pit wall. I was told later that Leeann thought I was sweet, which is the first time I've ever been called that!

Ben seems a typical Californian, very laid back although he takes his preparation seriously. He is always mixing high-energy drinks and eats a high protein diet right up until race day. I tend to eat what I want – although I won't touch alcohol for about a week before a race – and I discovered oysters for the first time at Montego Bay. The next day, Ben had an upset stomach and I felt fine. He's a talented rider who was bound to go fast at some tracks, but I also felt that he would struggle on others.

Thursday was also the day of the pre-meeting press conference. The FIM told us about some new fines and Chili stood up as usual to do his grandfather bit. He has a point, though. These things are always imposed on the riders without any discussions. Riders should have a representative on the governing bodies. But the most bizarre question came from one journalist who asked, 'Why do all the riders wear their sunglasses on their heads?' The answer is obvious, because most of us are sponsored to wear them.

My shades are provided by Oakley, and I had already done them one favour that year. For Christmas, Michaela bought me a solid gold Oakley watch that weighed a ton. The strap was too big for my wrist at first and I had to have a couple of links removed. This proved handy for Oakley as Mike Tyson bought the same watch when he was in Manchester to fight Julius Francis. But his strap was not big enough to fit round his wrist so we gave them back the links to add to his watch.

I bought Michaela some diamond earrings. Her presents get more and more expensive every year, but what do you buy someone who has everything? One year I bought her a solid gold Rolex and put it in a massive box filled with rags and her knickers. I videoed her searching for the small box, which was wrapped in wallpaper and stuck together with duct tape. Her face was a picture.

It was actually getting quite difficult fitting all the sponsors' badges on my leathers. But I had just done a deal with Motorbikes4U, a company that I had invested some money in along with a few other riders like Barry Sheene, to wear their new caps that advertised my new web site www.foggy-no1.com. I also stuck a small strip across the top of my visor because, due to the problems I'd had with Brian, it was important to get the message across that I now had an authentic official site.

In the first free practice session on Friday morning I had a few suspension problems and Edwards was quickest, with Haga also going well. He always seems to be good early in the season when his Dunlop tyres suit the first few circuits. I did 18 laps and the shoulder was still troubling me at three points on the circuit – two chicanes where I had to flip the bike over quickly and at one hard-braking corner. In the first qualifying session that afternoon, we tried some new forks because the track seemed bumpier than the previous year and they seemed a lot better. I also used a 16.5in tyre, which I had never raced on before. I haven't liked it in the past but it felt good and I reduced the difference between Edwards' fastest lap from 1.5 to just 0.3 seconds.

I would probably have gone quicker than him if a slow rider hadn't got in my way on my last lap.

It was another long day at the track, with a lot more physiotherapy on the shoulder plus more injections. After each session there was also a technical meeting with the engineers to discuss plans for the next day. And the BBC also wanted to do a piece with their presenter Suzi Perry, out on the track before the light faded. The very fact that it was their first race added to the pressure on me because I was aware that a lot more people would be watching back home. By the time we left the track in our hire car it was dark. You are always fairly nervous driving around over there, as the latest crime wave is car-jacking. So, when we drove past some flashing police lights at the side of the road, with what looked like a dead body sprawled out in the middle of the road, we didn't stop to see if it had been a shooting or a car accident!

In Saturday morning's final qualifying session I tried the tyre again and finished third fastest behind Edwards and Chili's Suzuki. But I was beginning to feel like I was going round in circles with all the different things we were trying and it might have been better to put the bike back to how it had been set up the previous year. My shoulder was not much better but I needed full movement in it during the final free practice of Saturday afternoon to give the finger to a slow guy called Massimo De Silvestro, who could have killed me when he turned straight into my path while pulling into the pit lane. I had to swerve just to miss running in the back of him. It was no surprise to me when Corser clinched Superpole. He's probably the best rider at doing one fast lap and Dunlop also produce a special tyre for it. I was third, just under a tenth of a second slower than Edwards, so at least I was on the front row of the grid at a track which is difficult to pass on.

It had already been a trying week. For these long-haul meetings, there was no point in Ducati bringing over the full hospitality set-up so we were all forced to share a room at the back of the garage. There was not much privacy and I even had to change into my leathers in front of everyone. After the press conference following Superpole, I just wanted to go through everything again with the mechanics to make sure we had covered all the bases before Sunday.

My mind was now totally on the racing. So it wasn't the best time for Ducati to have arranged a profile piece with *Sports Illustrated* at 6pm, just when I was ready to get back to the hotel room and shut myself away. Then there was a queue of autograph hunters waiting at the back of the garage with a pile of calendars to sign. Still, Michaela cheered me up when she rang her dad, then told me that Blackburn Rovers had won 5–0 and Manchester United beat West Ham 7–1. Michaela had a lot of time to kill at the track and she did her best to try and keep me as relaxed as possible in the build-up to a race. So she stayed in the room with me that night, instead of going out for a meal.

A crowd of nearly 60,000 turned up at the track for race day which, thankfully, turned out fine. That was twice the size of the previous year and four times that of the South African Grand Prix race the previous week at Welkom. A few Brits made the trip and had been shouting themselves hoarse, across the track from our garage on the finishing straight behind their English flags, for the previous two days. After morning warm-up I made my final visit to the *Clinica Mobile* to have about seven more injections in the shoulder area and a few pills. I almost tried a South African sports drink until one of the doctors told me at the last minute that it contained a banned substance. Looking back, that was a lucky escape because Haga tested positive for ephedrine at that meeting, which caused all sorts of problems all year with the authorities. But the doctors couldn't prevent some pain during the race, which soon boiled down to a three-way fight between Hagar, Edwards and me.

For the first time ever I used a 16.5in front tyre and the grip was not the best. Also, I was struggling to change gear and eventually had to do it manually, which used even more energy. And, while my top speed was good, I was losing some acceleration coming out of a few corners. So, on the last lap, I just wasn't able to make in-roads as Edwards won the race. I donated my trophy to the doctors at the track for putting up with me for the last few days, as I had not been the easiest person to deal with. It also saved me carrying the thing back on the plane!

In some ways, the result relaxed me for the second race because I probably couldn't have asked for much more, all things considered. But I got a terrible start and, after touching the back wheel of a Japanese rider called Haruchika Aoki, dropped down to eighth. I had swapped the front tyre back to a 17in and the grip was better, even though I lost the front end two or three times. Still, I managed to fight it and worked my way back up to the leading three pretty easily and was confident of getting past them with plenty of laps available.

Then, on the 11th lap, I lost the front end and slid into the gravel. The bike was still running and I tried to get back on but the gear lever was snapped and the brake line severed. So that was that. I had a mountain to climb so early in the season as Haga went on to win and join Edwards on 45 points, while I had just 16. Maybe I should have just ridden round the problem with the front end and settled for fourth. But that's just not me.

Luckily, we had brought our flights back to England a day forward, keen to get back home and surprise the girls.

There wasn't a lot of time to spare so I was able to get away from all the stupid questions and just hibernate with Michaela, who knows exactly how to handle me after a bad result. Danielle burst into tears again when her mum picked her up from school on Monday afternoon. But there was only a gap of less than two weeks before we were off to Australia and Japan for back-to-back rounds.

I have always had problems sleeping in the build-up to races, and especially in Australia because of the jetlag. So this year we decided to go out a couple of days early and visit Sydney, somewhere we've never been before. What a shithole! Everyone goes on about how fantastic a place it is but it pissed down most of the time we were there and, if you're like me and not into sightseeing, there's not much to do. It's not as though I'm going to queue up for tickets to see something at the Sydney Opera House. We had a look round the aquarium and took a couple of ferries around the harbour but I was glad to get away, especially when, for the first time in Australia, people started coming up and asking for autographs in the street. To make up for the disappointment, we decided to book a couple of days up on the Great Barrier Reef near Cairns on the way up to Japan, to try and see a bit of real Australia, as there was a chance we might never get back there.

The frustrating thing, though, was that the plan to get me into an Australian sleep pattern hadn't worked. I'd had about one decent night's sleep and was knackered by the time we made it down to Phillip Island, a couple of hours' drive from Melbourne. South Africa had been difficult for Michaela because there had not been many of the girls around. But Leeann had decided to fly over to see Ben, Troy's girlfriend Sam and Aaron Slight's wife, Megan, were there, and Michaela's best mate on the circuit, Andrea Cooke, was back on the scene as Jamie was racing in the

Supersport series. But, even with all the gossip that lot produces, I still wasn't sleeping well.

So, the evening after qualifying, Barry Sheene had a quiet word with me and suggested I tried taking a Valium tranquiliser. I wasn't so sure. People think you're a looney when you say you're on sleeping pills. But he swore by them and said that the Formula One driver Gerhard Berger always used to take them before races. I asked the doctors and they told me not to go near them. But it had been a difficult first day. A wet morning had prevented me doing more than five laps but I still managed to set the fastest lap. The wind was so strong in the afternoon that I was continually fighting it just to pull the bike in, which aggravated my shoulder, and I finished that qualifying session third fastest. As usual, I was totally wrapped up in the racing and finding it really difficult to relax. So I decided to give one of the pills a go that night and slept like a log.

I felt great the next morning and was fastest by a long way in the final morning qualifying session. That meant I was last out for Superpole. Just as I started the lap, I saw a few spots of rain on my visor and completely lost the plot. I panicked and rode round like there was a wasp in my helmet, trying to get the lap out the way before the rain set in. I was still quick in a couple of sections but was only sixth fastest, which meant a second row start for race day when more rain was predicted. For good measure, I took another Valium that night and slept better than I usually do.

As feared, the Sunday was wet and windy. If it had been a dry race I would have won without a problem because I was riding so well. We initially decided to use full wet weather tyres but changed them at the last minute to intermediates. As it turned out, it would have been better to stick with them because local rider, Anthony Gobert, used his local knowledge of the weather and won by a mile on wets. He was a bit lucky, though, because at one point it looked as though I might be able to claw back his 33-second lead.

The track had started to dry, which was destroying his wet weather tyres and I was gaining a couple of seconds a lap with enough of the race left to catch him. Just then it started to rain again and I had to concentrate on staying upright to collect a comfortable second place.

The showers held off towards the start of the second race at 3.30pm and it was declared 'dry'. That meant that, once the race was started, the result would stand if more than two-thirds of the laps were completed should it have started raining again. So this time we nearly all went with the same tyre combination, a cut intermediate on the front and a slick on the rear. With that decision made, I could concentrate on the job in hand, knowing that my British fans were crawling out of their beds early on Easter Sunday morning to watch the live coverage. Some stupid cow tried to get my autograph while the bike was started and revved up by the mechanics, as I sat next to a fan at the back of the garage to keep cool. But she was stopped by some of the team. I would've just ignored her anyway because, by then, I was in my own bubble.

I had been in this position hundreds of times, but it was always tense. After taking our positions on the grid, Luca and the other mechanics spent the final ten minutes checking that everything was okay and putting the warmers on the tyres to make sure they stayed heated. Michaela stood alongside me holding the umbrella to keep the sun, which kept bursting through the clouds, off my head. The photographers and television crews buzzed around, getting their final close-up pictures of my piercing blue eyes. Some riders allowed interviews – but the reporters knew better than to even ask me. That famous Foggy stare was fixed on the track ahead as the hooter sounded and the grid was cleared of everyone but the riders. Michaela was last to leave me. She hugged me and told me that she loved me. And her last words, always the same, were ... 'Come back!'

# *Career Record*

## 1983

| Venue/Race | Class | Place |
|---|---|---|
| Aintree | Formula 500 | 2nd, disqualified |
| Ouston | Formula 500 | 2nd, 1st |
| Mallory | Formula 500 | 1st, 2nd, 1st |
| Cadwell | Formula 500 | crashed |
| Mallory | Formula 500 | 1st |
| Oulton | 1000cc | 4th |
| Aintree | Formula 500 | 1st |
| Cadwell | Formula 500 | 1st |

....................................................................

## 1984

| Venue/Race | Class | Place |
|---|---|---|
| Snetterton | 250cc | retired |
| Thruxton (ACU) | 250cc | 10th |
| Cadwell | 250cc | 2nd, 3rd |
| | trophy | 6th |
| Donington (ACU) | 250cc | crashed |
| Oulton | 250cc | 5th |
| | 350cc | 5th |
| Oulton (ACU) | 250cc | 12th (heat) |
| Cadwell (ACU) | 250cc | 1st, retired |
| | 1000cc | 3rd |
| Aintree | 250cc | 2nd |

| Venue/Race | Class | Place |
|---|---|---|
| Mallory | 250cc | 1st, 1st |
|  | trophy | 1st |
| Cadwell | 250cc | 8th |
| Aintree | 250cc | 1st |
|  | 350cc | 9th |
| Carnaby (ACU) | 250cc | 5th |
| Oulton | 250cc | 1st |
|  | champs | 3rd |
| Mallory | 250cc | 5th |
| Silverstone (ACU) | 250cc | 4th |
| Aintree | 250cc | 1st |
|  | 350cc | 1st (heat) |
| Oulton | 250cc | 12th (heat) |
| Cadwell | 250cc | 1st |
|  | 350cc | 2nd |

......................................................................

## 1985

| Venue/Race | Class | Place |
|---|---|---|
| Oulton | 250cc | 1st |
|  | 350cc | 2nd |
|  | 500cc heat | 1st |
| Cadwell | 250cc | crashed |
| Snetterton: Sat | 250cc | 1st, 1st |
|  | 350cc | 4th, 4th |
| Snetterton: Sun (ACU) | 250cc | retired |
|  | 350cc | retired |
| Darley | 250cc | 1st |
|  | 350cc | 3rd (ACU Star) |
| Donington | 250cc | crashed |
| Oulton | 250cc | 6th |
| Aintree | 250cc | 1st |
|  | 350cc | 1st (heat) |
| Thruxton (ACU) | 250cc | 1st |

| Venue/Race | Class | Place |
|---|---|---|
| Brands (ACU) | 250cc | 7th |
| | 350cc | 8th |
| Mallory | 350cc | crashed |
| Cadwell (ACU) | 250cc | 6th |
| Aintree | 250cc | 1st (heat) |
| | 350cc | 1st |
| Lydden: Sat | 250cc | 1st |
| | 1000cc | 4th |
| Lydden: Sun (ACU) | 250cc | 1st |
| Donington: Sat | 250cc | 3rd |
| Donington: Sun (ACU) | 250cc | 9th |
| Aintree | 250cc | 1st |
| | 350cc | 1st |
| Mallory | 250cc | retired |
| Aintree | 250cc | 1st |
| | 350cc | 1st |
| Carnaby (ACU) | 250cc | 4th |
| Mallory (ACU) | 250cc | 11th |
| Manx GP | 250cc new-comers | 3rd and 1st |
| Aintree | 250cc | 1st |
| | 350cc | 2nd |
| Silverstone (ACU) | 250cc | 1st |
| Cadwell | 250cc | 9th |
| Darley | 250cc | 1st |

........................................................................

## 1986

| Venue/Race | Class | Place |
|---|---|---|
| Oulton | 250cc | 1st |
| | 350cc | 1st |
| Cadwell | 250cc | 7th, 8th |
| Brands | 250cc | 11th, 5th |

| Venue/Race | Class | Place |
|---|---|---|
| Donington | 250cc | 3rd |
| | Formula 2 | 1st |
| Oulton | 250cc | 6th |
| | 350cc | 2nd |
| | champs | 2nd |
| Cadwell | 250cc | 3rd |
| Thruxton | 250cc | 1st |
| | 350cc | crashed |
| Mallory | 250cc | retired |
| | Formula 2 | 2nd |
| Brands | 250cc | 2nd |
| Aintree | 250cc | 2nd |
| | 350cc | 1st |
| Isle of Man TT | 250cc | retired |
| | 350cc | retired |
| | 400cc | 17th |
| | 600cc | 12th |
| Mallory | 250cc | 2nd |
| Donington | 250cc | 4th, 5th |
| | Formula 2 | 1st |
| Aberdare | 250cc | 1st |
| | 1000cc | 1st |
| Scarborough: Sat | 350cc | 2nd |
| Scarborough: Sun | 250cc | 1st |
| Snetterton | 250cc | 2nd, 2nd |
| Mallory | 250cc | 2nd |
| British GP | 250cc | 11th |

........................................................................

# 1987

| Venue/Race | Class | Place |
|---|---|---|
| Jerez | 250cc | did not qualify |
| Donington | 250cc | did not qualify |
| Scarborough | 250cc | 1st |
| | 350cc | 1st |
| North West 200 | 250cc | crashed |
| Isle of Man TT | 350cc Junior | 4th |
| | 750cc | 9th |
| Donington | 350cc Super 2 | retired |
| | King of Don-ington | 4th |
| Aberdare | 250cc | 1st |
| | 1000cc | 1st |
| Cadwell | 350cc Super 2 | 4th |
| Scarborough: Sat | 250cc | 1st |
| | 350cc Super 2 | 1st |
| Scarborough: Sun | 250cc | 1st |
| | 1000cc | 5th |
| Knockhill | 350cc Super 2 | 2nd |
| | 1000cc | 9th (heat) |
| Snetterton | 350cc Super 2 | 5th |
| Mallory | 250cc | 1st |
| | 350cc Super 2 | 1st |
| British GP | 250cc | did not qualify |
| Thruxton | 250cc | 3rd, 4th |
| | 350cc Super 2 | 1st |
| Mallory | 250cc | 1st |
| | 1000cc | 5th |
| Scarborough: Sat | 350cc Super 2 | 1st |
| Scarborough: Sun | 250cc | 1st |
| Silverstone | 250cc | crashed |

# 1988

| Venue/Race | Class | Place |
|---|---|---|
| Donington | 250cc | did not finish |
| Thruxton | 250cc | 3rd |
| Scarborough | 250cc | 1st |
| | Superbikes | 3rd |
| Snetterton | 250cc | 2nd |
| Brands | 250cc | 7th |
| Pembrey | 250cc | 1st, 1st |
| | Superbikes | 3rd |
| North West 200 | 250cc | 2nd |
| | Superbikes | 5th |
| Carnaby | Formula One | 9th |
| Isle of Man TT | 600cc Super 2 | 12th |
| | Formula One | 4th |
| | 1000cc Senior | 7th |
| Donington | 250cc | 6th (heat) |
| | Superbikes | 5th |
| Assen | Formula One | 9th |
| Aberdare | 250cc | 1st |
| | 1000cc | 1st |
| Cadwell | Formula One | 3rd |
| Vila Real | Formula One | retired |
| Knockhill | 250cc | 2nd |
| | Formula One | 6th |
| Kouvola | Formula One | 4th |
| Mallory | Formula One | 5th |
| Ulster GP | Formula One | 1st |
| Pergusa | Formula One | 1st |
| Donington | Formula One | 5th (world title) |
| Cadwell: Sat | Superbikes | 3rd |
| Cadwell: Sun | Formula One | 4th |
| Kirkistown | 1000cc | 1st, 2nd |

## 1989

| Venue/Race | Class | Place |
|---|---|---|
| Brands | Eurochallenge | 11th, 10th, 8th |
| Donington: Sun | Eurochallenge | 3rd, 2nd |
| Donington: Mon | WSB | 7th, 13th |
| | Eurochallenge | 11th, 2nd, 4th |
| Mallory | 1000cc | crashed |
| Castle Combe | 1000cc | 1st |
| Thruxton | 1000cc | did not finish |
| Sugo | Formula One | 13th |
| Mallory | Formula One | 5th |
| Isle of Man TT | 1000cc | 4th |
| | 125cc | 3rd |
| | Junior | 4th |
| | 750cc | 1st |
| Cadwell | Formula One | 1st |
| | Superbikes | 1st |
| Donington | Formula One | 2nd |
| | Other | 1st |
| Assen | Formula One | 1st |
| Vila Real | Formula One | 2nd |
| Kouvola | Formula One | 1st |
| Donington: Sun | Superbikes | 2nd |
| Donington: Mon | Superbikes | 2nd |
| Ulster GP | Formula One | 2nd (world title) |
| | Other | 1st |
| Thruxton | Formula One | 4th |
| Suzuka 8 hours | Endurance | 33rd |
| Mallory | Superbikes | 3rd |
| | Other | 4th |
| Scarborough: Sat | 250cc | 1st |
| | Other | 1st, 1st |
| Scarborough: Sun | 250cc | 1st |
| | Other | 1st, 1st |

| Venue/Race | Class | Place |
|---|---|---|
| Cadwell | Formula One | 1st |
| | Other | 2nd |
| Donington | Formula One | 1st |
| | Superbikes | 1st, 1st |
| Darley | Other | 1st, 1st |
| Kirkistown | 1000cc | 2nd |

## 1990

| Venue/Race | Class | Place |
|---|---|---|
| Daytona 200 | 1000cc | crashed |
| Jerez | WSB | 14th, retired |
| Donington | WSB | 6th, 6th |
| Sugo | Formula One | 5th |
| North West 200 | Superbikes | 2nd |
| Snetterton | Superbikes | did not finish |
| Isle of Man TT | Superbikes | |
| | Senior | 1st |
| | Formula One | 1st |
| | 400cc | 2nd |
| | Junior | 4th |
| Donington | Superbikes | 3rd, 2nd |
| | Formula One | 1st |
| Vila Real | Formula One | 1st |
| Knockhill | Formula One | 1st |
| Kouvola | Formula One | 1st (world title) |
| Suzuka 8 hours | Endurance | crashed |
| British GP | 500cc | crashed |
| Swedish GP | 500cc | 6th |
| Czech GP | 500cc | 10th |
| Hungarian GP | 500cc | 8th |
| Oulton | Superbikes | 3rd, 1st |
| Cadwell | Superbikes | 8th, 1st |
| Le Mans | WSB | retired, 8th |

| Venue/Race | Class | Place |
|---|---|---|
| Donington | Formula One | 2nd |
| Kirkistown | 1000cc | 1st, 2nd |
| | Other | 2nd |
| Darley | Other | 1st, 1st |
| Brands | Superbikes | 3rd, 4th |
| | Formula One | |

..........................................................................

## 1991

| Venue/Race | Class | Place |
|---|---|---|
| Daytona 200 | | crashed |
| Donington: Sun | Formula One | retired |
| Donington: Mon | WSB | retired, 9th |
| Jarama | WSB | 9th, 8th |
| Mallory | (UK v USA) | 4th, 4th, 2nd |
| Brands | (UK v USA) | 7th, 7th, 9th |
| Donington | Formula One | 6th |
| | Supersport | 7th |
| Isle of Man TT | Formula One | 2nd |
| Brainerd | WSB | 11th, 11th |
| Brands | 1000cc | 8th |
| | Supersport | 6th |
| Cadwell | 1000cc | 2nd |
| | Supersport | 1st |
| Suzuka 8 hours | Endurance | 3rd |
| Misano | WSB | 7th, 8th |
| Anderstorp | WSB | 4th, 4th |
| Oulton | 1000cc | 3rd, 2nd |
| | Supersport 400 | 1st |
| Mallory | WSB | 11th, 8th |
| Sugo | 1000cc | 10th, 5th |
| Shah Alam | WSB | 8th, 7th |
| Hockenheim | WSB | 9th, 10th |
| Magny-Cours | WSB | 6th, 7th |

| Venue/Race | Class | Place |
|---|---|---|
| Mugello | WSB | 7th, retired |
| Kirkistown | 1000cc | 1st, 2nd |

......................................................................

## 1992

| Venue/Race | Class | Place |
|---|---|---|
| Albacete | WSB | 12th, 10th |
| Oulton | Superbikes | 2nd, 2nd |
| Donington | WSB | crashed, 1st |
| Le Mans | Endurance | 1st |
| Donington | 1000cc | 1st |
| Brands | 1000cc | did not finish |
| North West 200 | Superbikes | 4th |
| Hockenheim | WSB | retired, 11th |
| Spa | WSB | retired, 8th |
| Isle of Man TT | Senior | 2nd |
| Jarama | WSB | 5th, crashed |
| Spa | Endurance | 1st |
| Zeltweg | WSB | 6th, 7th |
| Snetterton | 1000cc | 6th |
| Mugello | WSB | 7th, 4th |
| Suzuka 8 hours | Endurance | did not finish |
| British GP | 500cc | crashed |
| Silverstone | Superbikes | 6th, 6th |
| Assen | WSB | 4th, 2nd |
| Bol d'Or | Endurance | 1st |
| Monza | WSB | retired, retired |
| Phillip Island | WSB | 7th, retired |
| | Endurance | 1st (world title) |
| Johor | Endurance | 1st |
| Macau GP | 1000cc | 1st |
| Malaysia | | 1st, 1st, retired |

......................................................................

## 1993

| Venue/Race | Class | Place |
|---|---|---|
| Brands | WSB | crashed |
| Hockenheim | WSB | 3rd, 7th |
| Oulton | Superbikes | retired, retired |
| North West 200 | Superbikes | 1st, 1st |
| Albacete | WSB | 1st, 1st |
| Donington | 1000cc | 1st, 1st |
| Misano | WSB | 5th, 3rd |
| Osterreichring | WSB | 4th, 4th |
| Brno | WSB | 1st, 2nd |
| British GP | 500cc | 4th |
| Anderstorp | WSB | 1st, 1st |
| Shah Alam | WSB | 1st, 1st |
| Sugo | WSB | 1st, crashed |
| Assen | WSB | 1st, 1st |
| Monza | WSB | 4th, 4th |
| Donington | WSB | 2nd, crashed |
| Estoril | WSB | crashed, 1st |
| Mexico | WSB | did not race |

## 1994

| Venue/Race | Class | Place |
|---|---|---|
| Donington | Superbikes | 1st, 1st |
| Donington | WSB | 1st, 3rd |
| Hockenheim | WSB | did not start |
| Misano | WSB | retired, 5th |
| Albacete | WSB | 1st, 1st |
| Zeltweg | WSB | 1st, 1st |
| British GP | 500cc | did not start |
| Sentul | WSB | retired, 1st |
| Sugo | WSB | 4th, 2nd |
| Assen | WSB | 1st, 1st |
| San Marino | WSB | 2nd, 1st |

| Venue/Race | Class | Place |
|---|---|---|
| Donington | WSB | 14th, 5th |
| Phillip Island | WSB | 1st, 2nd (world title) |

## 1995

| Venue/Race | Class | Place |
|---|---|---|
| Daytona | | 2nd |
| Hockenheim | WSB | 1st, 1st |
| Misano | WSB | 2nd, 2nd |
| Donington | WSB | 1st, 1st |
| Monza | WSB | 1st, 2nd |
| Albacete | WSB | 2nd, 1st |
| Salzburgring | WSB | 1st, 2nd |
| Laguna Seca | WSB | 5th, 7th |
| Brands | WSB | 1st, 1st |
| Sugo | WSB | crashed, 1st |
| Assen | WSB | 1st, 1st (world title) |
| Sentul | WSB | 1st, retired |
| Phillip Island | WSB | 4th, 2nd |

## 1996

| Venue/Race | Class | Place |
|---|---|---|
| Misano | WSB | 7th, 6th |
| Donington | WSB | 9th, 7th |
| Hockenheim | WSB | 5th, 1st |
| Monza | WSB | 1st, 3rd |
| Brno | WSB | 2nd, 3rd |
| Laguna Seca | WSB | 8th, 4th |
| Suzuka 8 hours | | 3rd |
| Brands | WSB | 5th, crashed |
| Sentul | WSB | 2nd, 3rd |
| Sugo | WSB | 8th, 4th |
| Assen | WSB | 1st, 1st |

| Venue/Race | Class | Place |
|---|---|---|
| Albacete | WSB | 5th, 7th |
| Phillip Island | WSB | 4th, 6th |

## 1997

| Venue/Race | Class | Place |
|---|---|---|
| Phillip Island | WSB | 2nd, 4th |
| Misano | WSB | 3rd, 3rd |
| Donington | WSB | 2nd, 1st |
| Hockenheim | WSB | 4th, 1st |
| Monza | WSB | 3rd, 4th |
| Laguna Seca | WSB | 2nd, 2nd |
| Brands | WSB | crashed, 1st |
| A1 Ring | WSB | 1st, crashed |
| Assen | WSB | 2nd, 1st |
| Albacete | WSB | crashed, crashed |
| Sugo | WSB | 13th, crashed |
| Sentul | WSB | 3rd, 1st |

## 1998

| Venue/Race | Class | Place |
|---|---|---|
| Phillip Island | WSB | 1st, 3rd |
| Donington | WSB | 7th, 3rd |
| Monza | WSB | 6th, 2nd |
| Albacete | WSB | 9th, 1st |
| Nurburgring | WSB | 13th, 13th |
| Misano | WSB | 4th, 3rd |
| Kyalami | WSB | 2nd, 2nd |
| Laguna Seca | WSB | 5th, retired |
| Brands | WSB | 4th, 2nd |
| A1 Ring | WSB | 3rd, 2nd |
| Assen | WSB | 2nd, 1st |
| Sugo | WSB | 3rd, 4th (world title) |

## 1999

| Venue/Race | Class | Place |
|---|---|---|
| Kyalami | WSB | 1st, 1st |
| Phillip Island | WSB | 2nd, 2nd |
| Donington | WSB | 1st, 2nd |
| Albacete | WSB | 3rd, 3rd |
| Monza | WSB | 1st, 1st |
| Nurburgring | WSB | 1st, 15th |
| Misano | WSB | 1st, 1st |
| Laguna Seca | WSB | 5th, 4th |
| Brands | WSB | 19th, 4th |
| A1 Ring | WSB | 2nd, 4th |
| Assen | WSB | 1st, 1st |
| Hockenheim | WSB | 1st, 2nd (world title) |
| Sugo | WSB | 2nd, 5th |

## 2000

| Venue/Race | Class | Place |
|---|---|---|
| Kyalami | WSB | 3rd, crashed |
| Phillip Island | WSB | 2nd, crashed |

# Index